THE ART OF
BEAD
EMBROIDERY

JAPANESE-STYLE

—— 2 ——

MARGARET LEE

INSPIRATIONS

CONTENTS

PREFACE

'Creativity' is a natural next step for any embroiderer after acquiring technical and practical skills along with the underpinning knowledge of an embroidery style. Yet this is not often the case, and we hear contentions like 'I am not creative' or 'I do not have creative talent'.... and so forth.

Art and Craft in Asia, and its well-established system of passing on skills to the next generation, provides evidence that creativity can be developed and acquired in a structured manner. This is what this book aims to do. It provides insights and personal experiences with creativity and how conditions can be established to promote individual creativity.

A personal aim of my role as an embroidery teacher is to help develop and guide each student towards their individual creativity. Projects in this book demonstrate creativity in action and seek to also plant the seeds of creativity for all its readers.

ACKNOWLEDGEMENTS

This book is not just a how-to book with designs and projects to embroider. It also discusses progressive and practical means that help develop individual creativity, with projects that showcase this in action.

The ideas discussed are by no means exhaustive but have been shaped by wisdom passed down from elders that have gone before us on the embroidery journey; from a personal cultural background and lived experience and from all those who have mentored me and been an inspiration in my personal embroidery journey.

As always, there are many people that have made the vision for this book a reality.

Firstly, to my group of fellow embroidery enthusiasts who accepted the undertaking to pair their individual creative ideas to the projects in this book. Thank you, Marie Hansen, Cecilia Andersson, Sue Fox, Loic Jeanneau, Kay Jenkins, Barbara Roberts, Jacqueline Poirier, Robyn Ferrero, Frances Langenberg, Carol James and Razi Wight. You will see their creations and read about their individual experiences in the book.

The incredible dream team from Inspirations Studios who make every book beautiful and visions come true. Especial mention to the dynamic editorial pair, Susan O'Connor and Ellaine Bronsert who ensure that all the t's are crossed, and the i's are dotted. Thank you all for your support.

Acknowledgement and deep appreciation go to the Japanese Embroidery Centre, Atlanta and Kurenai-kai who planted the first seeds of *Nuido* outside Japan for the practice of Traditional Japanese Silk Embroidery and Bead Embroidery as its companion art. I pay deepest respect and gratitude to Reiko Matsukawa-san who has taught me not only the Art of Bead Embroidery but instilled in me the importance of passing on the art with utmost integrity.

Last, but not least, my love and gratitude to my beloved husband, David, my daughters, Yvonne, Yvette and Yolanda and grandchildren, Aiden, Olivia and Elizabeth. Thank you for hugs, laughter and special memories.

'Continue the self-discipline that has enabled you to reach this achievement and pass on the tradition in its integrity.'

This quote was on my graduation certificate issued by Reiko Matsukawa-san for Kurenai-kai Beads. As a practitioner of traditional Japanese embroidery and Chinese silk embroidery, that have roots dating back thousands of years, this resonates strongly with me. I am a self-professed traditionalist where these embroideries are concerned and have been fascinated with the traditions attached to them, through their development through history, their adaptation and progress with changes in societal practices, economics and government.

Looking back through history, Japanese embroidery techniques, designs, and practices have adapted and maintained their currency through different eras. At each level of change, a new dimension is added to the embroidery further enriching it. These changes are influenced or triggered by both domestic and external developments.

What, I ask, does it mean to continue the tradition that has been entrusted with the certificate? History has shown that embroidery is not static but updates and evolves. This set me on the path of developing within my teaching agenda an approach that not only teaches the techniques and practices, but looks to the next step, creativity. This must, however, be done in such a way that the integrity of the principles, practices and techniques of the art is not compromised.

Studying traditional Japanese silk embroidery under the aegis of Kurenai -kai and the Japanese Embroidery Centre, Atlanta, the concept of the three progressive pillars that underpin traditional silk embroidery (Nuido— The way of embroidery) is taught. It is not just learning with the mind but a development also of our senses and emotional understanding of the practice.

The first pillar we acquire is 'Rationality'. At this stage the basic principles, techniques and practices of traditional Japanese embroidery are acquired.

Through consistent practise muscle memory is developed and hand-eye co-ordination skills are honed.

The second pillar of 'Sensitivity' follows when we engage our senses and discern the intricacies involved with colours, patterns, designs, threads, and techniques that are unique to Japanese culture. To name a few: designs and colours reflect the Japanese delicate sense towards changing seasons and colours; the visual movement created by the arrangements of patterns and design elements, and symbolism of design arrangements.

The third pillar of 'Spirituality' results when a deep understanding of the first two pillars is achieved. This is the phase, in my opinion, when everything comes together in a holistic manner and the zone when creativity happens.

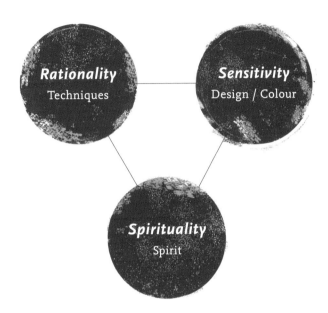

The Three Pillars of Japanese Embroidery

What is creativity? Is creativity inborn or can it be acquired? Can it be taught? There has been much research as well as debate on this over the decades. While no clear answer seems to have emerged, there have been many voices that advocate that creativity is a skill that can be developed.

The *Cambridge Dictionary* defines creativity as 'the ability to produce or use original and unusual ideas'. In this context it means that creativity can be applied to almost everything. How does this correlate to the historical development of Japanese embroidery? It cannot be said that it fits within the definition in its strictest form.

This is because, within Asian cultures, the concept of creativity is viewed from a different perspective. It is more akin to the Western concept of innovation, which is defined in the *Cambridge Dictionary* as 'a new method or idea'. It is centred around progressive improvement,

adjustment, and adaptation to new or changed circumstances or to overcome a perceived impediment. It also focusses on innovating or perfecting an existing idea and progressively refining it. It is the catalyst that saw the transformation of the status of embroidery in China from craft to high art. It is the same catalyst that underpinned the currency of embroidery through the various eras of Japanese history. We see popular traditional designs commonly used across different arts and crafts, with each discipline producing unique items within their domain. It is through this Asian lens that the subject of creativity is discussed in this book.

Outside of embroidery, it is worth mentioning that this same catalyst drove post-war Japanese industrial activities and businesses to new heights, a process known as *kaizen* or 'continuous improvement'. It proved so successful that the concept and practices spread to other countries.

This seeded the idea to include the topic of creativity, Asian-style of course, as part of my teaching. Not only should my teaching include the practical and sensory part of the embroidery, it should lead fellow embroidery enthusiasts to develop their personal creativity as the next step. It felt right as Japanese-style bead embroidery is itself the fruit of such creativity when Mr Iwao Saito developed the idea of substituting beads for silk threads, underpinned by techniques associated with traditional silk embroidery. It came at a time that saw an increase in both domestic and international markets for beaded accessories, particularly bags. It resulted in a unique bead embroidery style that embodies the intrinsic features produced in silk embroidery—movement, texture and perspective, both dimensional and linear.

In the first book, *The Art of Bead Embroidery*, the focus was on practical aspects of, and the underpinning techniques and principles of, the art. It also introduced conceptual ideas behind its practice. Projects offered in the book aimed to introduce and develop technical and practical skills while preparing for the next step to creativity.

In this second book, we now explore ideas on developing and enhancing creativity in embroidery from an Asian perspective. I have long espoused the precept that, at some point in a tutor-student relationship, the tutor's role shifts to that of a mentor to develop individual creativity. A quote from Albert Einstein is further encouragement and reminder of this responsibility.

'It is the supreme art of the teacher to awaken joy in creative expression and knowledge.'

It is important to recognise that the ideas in this book are not based on any academic research but are drawn from a cultural perspective, lived experience, and personal experiences in the corporate world and as an embroidery practitioner, teacher, and designer.

Creativity can be segregated into a macro and micro level. At the macro level, creativity is developed and polished, while at the micro level, creativity is applied in practice to the creation of designs and/or interpretation of designs to create a unique embroidered item.

Many different factors can contribute to and improve creativity. I share below some key concepts and habits that have facilitated me in this sphere.

PRACTISE, PRACTISE, AND MORE PRACTISE

'Practise isn't the thing you do once you're good. It's the thing you do that makes you good.'

This is a quote from '*Outliers*' by Malcolm Gladwell. In his book, Gladwell espouses the rule of 10,000 hours, which is backed by research. This rule suggests that mastery of a skill can be achieved through 10,000 hours of effort and practise. Examples cited range from the Beatles to Bill Gates and it makes an interesting read.

The theory appears to be supported by the traditional Japanese apprentice system in many areas of craft, including embroidery, where the road to professional status generally spans over five years or more. It is a highly disciplined path with little vacation and often long hours. At a conservative estimate of a 40-hour week, this equates to the 10,000 hours theory.

From the embroidery perspective, practise is vital. The more we do, the more comfortable we become with the techniques and underlying principles of the embroidery style. The more comfortable we are, the more we begin to see beyond the practise and start to think creatively. Muscle memory is firmly established, stitching is intuitive and set to 'automatic'. Hand-eye co-ordination is also well developed. A phenomenon that will transpire in the subconscious is the way designs and patterns are viewed. A discerning shift from 'seeing' to 'perceiving' a design or pattern emerges. Instead of a two-dimensional view of outlines and patterns, the way objects, designs and patterns are perceived will include a third dimension where colours, movement, texture, and perspective spontaneously emerge. The shift into the creative mode has begun.

BE INSPIRED BY NATURE

Nature is one of our greatest teachers of colours and shapes. Register colours of flora and fauna as you see them in nature. The colour combination that abounds in nature is never wrong and always perfect in every situation. See the magical colour harmony in different bird species, flowers, and plants, colour contrasts, shades, and tints. See the same in earth, sea and sky at different times of the day and in different weather conditions. Observe also colour changes through the different seasons and geographic areas. As you observe and in turn perceive, ideas form and creativity will take its natural course. Catalogue anything you see that appeals for future reference. With the mobile phones of today, instant records can be created for your personal visual library.

BE INSPIRED BY OTHER ARTISTIC PRACTICES

Artistry and creative expressions abound across many disciplines - handicrafts, visual arts, architecture, landscaping, pottery, tiles, bonsai cultivation, to name but a few. Observe parallels between these and your embroidery practice. Look at colour combinations, patterns and shapes and their arrangements. Perhaps there is something that can be incorporated into your design or adapted to your embroidery.

Later in the book, we will see this in action where Japanese embroidery, goldwork and yuzen dyeing ideas are borrowed and adapted to apply alongside bead embroidery.

BE INSPIRED BY HISTORY

History provides us with an abundance of inspiration from varied textile designs and patterns as well as artistic development of different historical periods. Here are a few examples of creative ideas from the past that lend themselves to bead embroidery. Take a walk back into history and be amazed and inspired by what you find.

17th century Jacobean textile designs that feature stylised floral patterns and fruits are a great source for creative inspiration. The typically flowing movement of these designs is almost a perfect fit for Japanese-style bead embroidery as movement is one of the key underlying principles.

Wassily Kandinsky, born 16 December 1866, is considered to have pioneered abstract painting in the early 20th century with typically geometric forms and lines and a strong focus on colour and texture. His art form was one of the major influences for the later Art Deco style. A project in this book is inspired by his art.

Wagara, some of which date as far back as the 5th century, are traditional Japanese patterns that are steeped in tradition and have highly symbolic meanings attached to them. They are also great a source for design ideas. The project in this book, *Shippo Flowers*, is based on a *wagara*. Another project, *Noshi*, includes not only *wagara* patterns but also patterns that are highly symbolic.

When designs and patterns are viewed from a historical perspective, they take on new meaning as we create with them. The final design will have its own story to tell.

BE INSPIRED BY OTHER CULTURES AND THEIR ARTS

This is a favourite of mine arising from a personal interest in tradition, cultural practices, and all things historical. Every culture has their unique creative expressions that reflect the unique customs and norms of their society as they change and evolve through history. The architecture, artworks, textiles, and objects of everyday life of different cultures provide limitless inspiration, not only in designs and patterns but also the way colours are perceived. In many cultures, designs and patterns also contain deeper meanings and symbolism.

Caution is advised when adapting ideas from another culture. Detailed research and understanding of an idea, design, or pattern within the context of the culture is recommended to avoid incorrect use of design ideas or colours that may cause offence.

BRAINSTORMING AND SECOND OPINIONS

In the creative process, one can sometimes be too close to the subject and hit a creative bump, where an idea is brewing but remains elusive and just beyond reach. Brainstorming with embroidery friends might just trigger the missing link to bring the idea to fruition.

As ideas form and a design emerges, aspects of the design that were initially considered to be a great idea may now look to be a misfit. There will be the inclination to hang on to them stubbornly given that they were the initial seeds for the design. I have been in this position many times and have learnt that not only is it a barrier to the successful transition of ideas into a final design, but it is a time-waster. Be brutal – listen to your inner voice that is backed by the pillars of rationality and sensitivity and discard early.

Do not hesitate to test your ideas and seek second opinions. Discover which part of the design others like – this is likely the part that does not require change. Work on improving the parts that did not impress. Determine suggestions that you like and wish to consider, then act on them. In the process, the design will be refined.

CORRECT MINDSET

Creativity is often spontaneously triggered by something that we see. Sight is by far the most common trigger, however, do not be surprised if the idea involves your other senses. A smell can evoke the image of something associated with it. The textural feel of a surface can also do the same as does a sound or taste. Embrace the moment and create – put up the 'Do not Disturb' sign if necessary.

Conversely, creativity cannot be forced and the equivalent of a 'writer's block' can happen. Look for inspiration from your library of images, brainstorm or go through any number of processes that have previously helped. If all else fails, walk away – frustration will make it worse and is not productive. Take a walk, read a book or get involved with something totally unrelated. Allow the subconscious to reset itself.

BE BRAVE

Take the leap. There is no right or wrong so long as you maintain the underpinning principles dictated by the embroidery style and due diligence is done to ensure that the design and its components do not cause offence and are culturally and historically appropriate.

With a view of creativity at the macro level, creativity moves to the micro level where creation of designs and embroidery begin. Decisions are made to bring the design to fruition, and these include the selection of beads, the decision on techniques to apply, colour selection and other embroidery decisions. Variation to any of these can result in very different outcomes and this will be demonstrated in the project section.

THE '5Ws'

We were taught in school that we have 5 best friends in the English language when writing a story **Who, What, Where, When and Why**. To these five friends,

I will add a sixth, **How.** These same best friends for story writing are also best friends for creativity at the micro level. Conversations with them will lead us in a systematic and logical manner to answers that we seek. The order in which we ask these questions depends on circumstances, but they always lead to an answer.

What?

A good starting point are the questions:

What is the proposed project?
e.g., box top, evening bag, purse etc.

What is the proposed size?

What is the proposed shape?

What is its purpose?

These three **What** questions on project, size and shape set the parameters for the size and style of designs that may suit the project and the purpose helps determine a design that suits the occasion.

Who?

Who is the project for? This is important as the identification of the intended recipient will provide the information on personal preferences and narrow down suitable design options and colour considerations. This is significant in Japanese culture as designs and colours have deeply rooted values.

Designs and colours reflect the Japanese delicate sense towards changing season and colours.

Designs and colours also reflect 'dignity' associated with the age of the wearer and context of occasion.

Designs embody underlying visual messages, often prescribed by the occasion, season and standing.

Once the design is complete, colour planning and technique selection take place. This step sees a return to the **What** question followed by **Why.**

Youthful

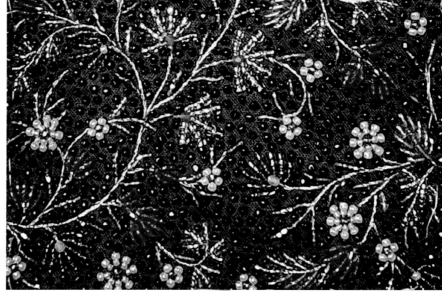

Mature

What and Why – Colour planning

What colour scheme will be suitable for the design? If a broad colour vision can be established, detailed colour selection becomes easier. Colour decisions could be a cool palette, warm palette, tone on tone etc.

Why is this colour scheme selected? The answer to this may be associated with culture, such as that mentioned for Japanese culture, it could be based on the design context or some other underlying considerations. If an answer is forthcoming, detailed colour planning comes easily as there are fundamental reasons for its selection. This is underpinned by the second pillar of sensitivity. If an answer does not exist, then it is back to the drawing board.

Detailed colour planning can be quite involved for complex designs. For such designs, a useful method is to create a colour chart by colouring the line drawing with coloured pencils. This presents an opportunity to view colour balance and combinations within the design. It also facilitates an overview of linear and dimensional perspective created by the proposed colour combinations and shading.

What and why – Technique and bead selection

With a detailed colour plan, the following can be discerned:

Relative prominence of different design elements. Different techniques can then be selected and applied to the design elements to ensure the integrity of the overall design. The technique choices will be augmented by considered selection of bead sizes and colour contrast. For textural contrast, bead type and finishes provide the effect.

Movement for overall design: colour will be key to maintaining the movement of the design as it leads the visual flow.

Linear and dimensional perspective: technique, colour, and bead size will create the required perspective. In addition, use of negative space will enhance the effect.

As with colour planning, the choice of technique, beads and colour for each element must also answer the question **Why**.

This systematic and progressive planning of a design from a macro level through to the micro level will enable us to make the best choices for the design at every step and ultimately produce a project that is meaningful and encompasses all the elements of movement, texture and perspective associated with Japanese-style bead embroidery.

In the project section of this book, I invited fellow embroidery enthusiasts to share their creativity in design, colours, and projects. The results are examples of different aspects of creativity in action and show the diverse creative potential that exists in each of us.

BEADS

Beads are available to the embroiderer in diverse materials, shapes, sizes and finishes. As we primarily use seed beads in Japanese-style bead embroidery, this will be the bead type we focus our discussion on.

What then do we look for when selecting beads for embroidery?

MATERIALS

At a glance, all beads look much the same but the shine they produce is different. Beads made from synthetic materials have comparatively less shine, can suffer from wear and tear and, generally, will deteriorate over time. If made from plastic, they may also be susceptible to accidental melting when ironed.

Glass and crystal beads do not share many of the problems associated with beads made from synthetic materials. Of these, crystal beads are limited in colour and are more costly but, how they sparkle! They are useful for that special highlight that you might like to add and complement glass beads well.

That leaves glass beads, which are the bead of choice for Japanese-style bead embroidery. The range of colours available in graduated sizes and finishes leaves the embroiderer spoilt for choice. Japanese beads are available in the common sizes from 3–15, with the larger number corresponding to the smaller size for the bead. Certain finishes can be affected by sunlight and friction and these should always be highlighted by the manufacturer.

The Czech Republic produces glass seed beads that are also suitable. These beads have some characteristics that are different from Japanese beads and their selection will be based on the effect that one may wish to create for the project.

BEAD SIZES

Bead sizes follow standard parameters and are usually categorised as a number against /0, e.g. 11/0 refers to size 11 beads. The 0 refers to a standard bead size against which all other sizes are referenced, e.g. 11/0 refers to a bead size that is 11 times smaller than the standard 0 size. This categorisation results in a bead sizing system where the larger the number, the smaller the bead.

While there are historical reasons for this categorisation it is not absolutely clear cut. It has been credited to both the size of the rods used in bead making, as well as to the number of beads that make up an inch placed in a row.

Bead sizes can be confusing and often we find actual physical size differences in beads of the same referenced size between manufacturers and even from the same manufacturer. This is due to the fact that different finishes, some of which add additional coatings or layers to the bead, can change the size. As a result, size 11 beads, the most common size used in bead embroidery, can vary in size from 1.8mm-2.2mm.

The bead embroiderer should be aware of this anomaly and ensure that the actual size of the beads selected are suitable for the project in hand.

SIZE CONSISTENCY

This is a crucial factor as inconsistent sizing will distort the 'movement' that we are trying to create. If the sizes are consistent, an even effect will be created that is pleasing to the eye.

Beads from China and India tend to be less uniform than the Japanese and Czech beads. Note also that the size of the beads manufactured in different countries can vary even though they may be given the same size number. For example, for the same size reference,

Japanese beads are slightly longer and have a larger hole than Czech seed beads, which are more donut shaped.

SHAPE

Seed beads are available in different shapes with more being added as manufacturers innovate in this area in response to market dictates. The most commonly used shapes are:

Round: These have nicely rounded edges and are smooth to the touch. They are the mainstay of Japanese-style bead embroidery.

Hexagon: These are faceted beads with six sides as the name suggests. The facets are even around the circumference of the bead

3–cut: These have random cuts to the surface of each bead. As a result they sparkle more as the light reflects off the surface at different levels and angles, giving each bead movement. Japanese 3-cut beads generally start with a round bead shape to which the cuts are made. Czech beads go through the same process but start out as a hexagonal bead giving a more elongated look. *Toho* 3-cut beads are sold in four sizes and use the following manufacturer's codes: size 8 – CRL, size 9 – CRM, size 12 – CR and size 15 – CRS. Czech 3-cut beads are only referenced by size and are available in size 9 and size 12.

Bugle: These are long thin tubes with flat ends and are available in lengths from 2mm–40mm. Despite the long shape, they are grouped in the seed bead category. Within bugle beads there are many variations. To name a few, bugle beads can be smooth with a round hole, twisted smooth with a square hole, hexagon bugle with a round hole, twisted hexagon bugle with a square hole. The ones that we

commonly use are 2mm and 3mm smooth bugle beads with round holes.

2–cut: These beads are similar to bugle beads. They have flat sides that give off a reflective sparkle. Sizing starts from 1.5mm.

FINISHES

Seed beads can be finished in a variety of ways, each exhibiting a different visual effect. This provides the embroiderer with a wide range of possibilities for projects. It is much like selecting threads and colours for embroidery. Finishes are usually the last part of the bead making process and some are unique to certain types of beads or to an individual manufacturer. It is therefore impossible to list all that are available in the market.

As is the case with bead shapes and shape refinements, the coatings and finishes that are applied to beads are another area where continuous innovation comes into play.

As with any applied coatings and finishes there is the possibility of fading through long exposure to sunlight, or wear through day to day use. However this is now far more likely with cheap seed beads from India and China than with the four main seed bead manufacturers. They have all added a final firing stage into their process to ensure their coatings and finishes are as durable as they can be. As has been the case throughout history, the formulas and processes used in glass production remain a closely guarded secret.

A broad range of beads is available to the bead embroiderer. This is both exciting and daunting, especially when considering that this list is not exhaustive. In this, my advice will be to go back to the basic question – What look do I wish to create for this project? From that vantage point, choose the right beads for your project.

The following techniques utilised in the projects in this book are new. The techniques used in these projects from book 1 begin on page 133.

Here we look at two Japanese handiwork traditions that can be creatively combined with and adapted for Japanese-style bead embroidery. They are the goldwork techniques of traditional Japanese embroidery and *yuzen* dyeing.

JAPANESE GOLDWORK

Japanese goldwork techniques are a formal part of traditional Japanese embroidery and add opulence. Japanese goldwork uses primarily Jap gold, which is made up of a metal foil wrapped around a thread core. The type of thread core influences how the gold thread works and the best metal threads for Japanese goldwork have a silk core wound with strips of gold leaf paper. Threads with real gold are also available.

True to the meticulous attention to detail that artisans give to their craft, Japanese goldwork is no different. Apart from gold and silver threads, other coloured metal threads are also available providing the embroiderer with diverse artistic options. When goldwork is discussed, this also refers to other coloured metal threads as the handling of these threads and stitching with them are the same.

The first step to any high-quality work is understanding the materials, in this case the metal threads, being used. Metal threads come in different sizes. They are sized as no. 1, no. 2, no. 3, no. 4... and so forth. There is also a no. 0.8 sized thread available. What do these numbers mean? They are how we know the thickness of

the metal thread with no. 1 being the base size. No. 2 metal thread is therefore two times the thickness of no. 1; no. 3 metal thread is three times the thickness of no. 1, and so forth.

No. 1 metal thread is very close to machine metallic sewing thread. This is good to know as Japanese no. 1 metal thread for hand embroidery may not always be easily available. Machine metallic sewing thread can be substituted if the colour is right and there are some high-quality machine threads that are suitable for bead embroidery. *YLI, Madeira* metallics and *Robison-Anton J* metallics are recommended brands.

Japanese metal threads are Z-twist threads. This is important to know to ensure that the correct twist of the thread is maintained during stitching for

maximum shine. Being a Z-twist thread, the twist can be tightened by retwisting the thread in a counter-clockwise direction. Conversely, twisting the thread in a clockwise direction will loosen the twist of the thread.

The exception to this is twisted metal threads, which are supplied ready twisted. Two threads of the same size are twisted into one with an S-twist. For these threads therefore, twisting the thread clockwise will tighten the twist and twisting it counter-clockwise loosen it.

At all times during stitching, watch the thread closely to ensure that the correct twist is maintained. Tighten or loosen the twist of the thread as required to ensure maximum shine and even twists.

Metal threads are further categorised into the following two broad categories:

STITCHABLE METAL THREADS

These vary in sizes up to no. 2. As the name suggests, they are threaded through a needle and stitched. They are normally supplied in skeins except for machine metallic sewing threads that are supplied on spools. If threads are supplied in skeins, they are prepared and stored in paper sachets ready for stitching. The steps for this are as follows:

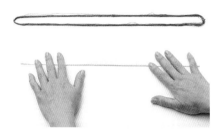

1 Take a piece of acid-free A3 paper and cut in half lengthwise. Fold lengthwise leaving one side 1cm (⅜") wider than the other. Open out the fold.

4 Continue folding over and over until all the paper is used. Tape the edge neatly.

2 Loop the skein of metal thread over one half of the paper and bring to rest along the fold. The end where the skein is tied should be exposed while the other end is level with the edge of the paper. Re-fold.

5 Cut through all the threads at the end where the skein is tied.

3 Fold the folded edge of paper approximately 1.5cm (⅝") from the previous fold, enclosing the remaining half of the skein.

6 At the looped end, pull out the strands as required, one at a time.

When stitching with metal threads, sizes up to no. 1 are half-hitched onto a needle before stitching commences. As the thread is usually stitched doubled, this helps to maintain good and even tension. Use a laying tool to help ensure the metal threads do not twist during stitching.

To half-hitch a metal thread, use a full length of gold thread and fold in half.

Bring the two cut ends of the thread together.

Thread both ends through the needle.

Gently slide the needle towards the looped end of the thread.

Take the needle through the loop and pull to secure the thread in a half-hitch.

No. 2 metal threads are used singly through the needle. If a double thread is required, knot the two ends together. For single threads, knot one end.

Special Japanese needles are usually used but these may be difficult to obtain. Suitable embroidery needles to use for stitchable metal threads include no. 24 and no. 26 chenille needles and no. 7 sharp.

NON-STITCHABLE METAL THREADS

These metal threads range in size from no. 3 upwards. They are couched either singly or in pairs in different ways to cover a shape or to create lines. Only the principles for couching single or a pair of non-stitchable metal threads, as used for projects in this book, are covered. Other variations are included in the instructions for the individual projects. A fine, twisted no. 100 silk thread is used to couch the metal threads.

Koma are used to help maintain good tension and ensure that gold threads lie smoothly on the surface of the fabric.

The first step towards beautiful, couched metal work is the correct winding of the metal threads onto a koma. A skein of metal thread is usually divided and wound onto two koma to facilitate couching pairs of non-stitchable metal threads. Begin winding the metal thread onto the first koma. When approximately at the halfway mark, cut the thread and continue to wind onto the second koma.

Working with koma

For good tension, the mantra when couching threads is: *stitch (work the couching stitch)..... tension (a small tug on the koma to even tension)..... position (the thread to the exact position for the next couching stitch)..... stitch..... etc. This applies to all couching using koma.*

Couching stitches are spaced 2mm–2.5mm (1/16"–3/32") apart depending on the curve – the tighter the curve the smaller the spacing. These stitches are also perpendicular to the metal thread being couched at the point of couching.

Metal threads are generally couched in pairs. Aside from straight lines, a pair of threads going around any curve means that the thread sitting on the outer side of the curve has a greater distance to travel than the inner one. The tighter the curve the greater the variance.

To maintain even tension on both threads, the koma are held in such a way that the two threads can be separately tensioned during the tension and position stages of the mantra. The way in which they are held will be determined by the direction that the threads are travelling. Pictured are examples of positions in which they are held. This may vary as each discovers their personal comfort positions.

Holding positions for koma during couching

Position 1

1 *Koma 1* – held between the little finger and below the base of the thumb of the left hand.

2 *Koma 2* – held between the thumb and second finger of the left hand.

3 Tension and position towards or to the left of the sitting position.

Position 2

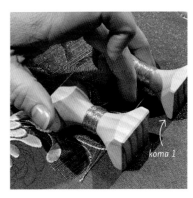

1 *Koma 1* – held between the second and third finger of the left hand.

2 *Koma 2* – held between the thumb and first finger of the left hand.

3 Tension and position away from the sitting position.

The following are general guidelines for couching non-stitchable metal threads.

COUCHING–PAIRS TECHNIQUE

Beginning and ending

- Where possible, begin at a corner in an unobtrusive position.

- When couching a pair of threads, position one metal thread over the design line at the starting point, leaving a 7mm (⁵⁄₁₆") tail. Anchor the thread with a couching stitch on the exact starting point. Lock in place with a pin stitch if desired.

- Position the second metal thread beside the first and couch over both threads, covering the previous couching stitch. If working with a single thread, omit this step.

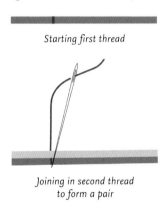

Starting first thread

Joining in second thread to form a pair

- Work the last couching stitch at the end point and trim the threads, leaving 7mm (⁵⁄₁₆") tails.

Sinking metal thread tails

Use the prepared sinking needle (see page 54). Where there is a pair of metal thread tails to take through to the back of the work, sink one at a time.

- Sink the ends of each thread in the pair separately.

- Insert the sinking needle through the fabric at the required point, at the first or last couching stitch.

- Insert the needle up to the eye and pass the end of the metal thread tail through the lasso of the sinking needle.

- Pull the needle through until the metal thread is held flat against the fabric by the lasso.

- Tension the metal thread with a gentle tug and pull the lasso taut.

- Trim the end of the metal thread tail to 3mm (⅛"). Holding the tail of the lasso with the needle, pull downwards on the sinking needle, using the lasso to take the metal thread tail through the fabric to the back of the work.

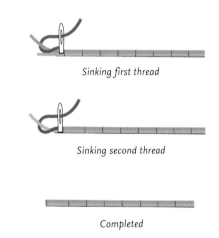

Sinking first thread

Sinking second thread

Completed

Turning metal threads at corners and points

Turning metal threads at corners and points of a design is likely the most challenging and important part of couching metal threads as it is the points and corners that provide definition to the shapes. The integrity of the points and corners must be maintained. It is also at these points that stress is placed on the metal thread as they are turned, so care must be taken that the twist of the thread is maintained, and the thread does not become distorted to the extent that the inner core thread becomes exposed.

The following practical considerations will help to avoid this:

- Exaggerate the points and corners. At points, stitch one point beyond the design line and for corners, stitch one point in from the design line. This will result in crisp points/corners and avoid these points and corners becoming rounded.

- The stitching sequence employed to turn metal threads at all corners and points is summarised below:

  i Work a couching stitch at the turning point. This is a stitch that must be at least one point smaller than the metal thread being couched. The stitch bisects the angle of the corner/point.

  ii Tension the metal thread being turned.

  iii Tighten tension on the couching stitch. Continue to maintain this tension with your left hand under the embroidery as the next steps proceed.

  iv With your right hand, pick up the koma and release a short length of thread. Open the twist of the metal thread by winding the thread back on the koma with several turns in a clockwise direction. Do this under tension. This opening up of the twist reduces the size of the thread and helps achieve a sharper point.

  v Turn the metal thread, exaggerating the turn slightly. You will note that part of the thread core will be exposed.

vi With the couching stitch still held firmly, close the twist of the metal thread by releasing a short length of thread, as necessary, and wind back on with several turns in a counter-clockwise direction. Note that this closes the twist and the thread core, previously exposed, will be covered over, leaving a neat point/corner.

vii Make a small pin stitch to lock the stitch in place.

viii Continue couching.

When couching a pair of metal threads, the threads are turned independently of each other at points or corners. When turning an outward point, the outer thread to the point has a longer distance to travel. Conversely, when turning an inward corner, it is the inner thread that has a longer distance to travel. Note that there are three stitches at every turning point or corner. The first two stitches turn the pair of metal threads independently and the third stitch brings the two threads together to continue couching as a pair. A graphical representation is given below:

Turning a point– pair of threads

Stitch one: Bisect the angle of the turn and turn the outer thread (diag 1).

Stitch two: Work over both threads before the point and turn the inner thread (diag 2).

Stitch three: Work over both threads after the point, sharing the hole of stitch two and forming a V shape (diag 3).

Turning a corner– pair of threads

Stitch one: Work over both threads and turn the inner thread (diag 4).

Stitch two: work over the outer thread only and turn the outer thread (diag 5).

Stitch three: Work over both threads, sharing the hole of stitch one and forming a V shape (diag 6).

Note the following:

- The couching stitch that turns the outer point bisects the angle of the turn.

- The angle of the two couching stitches that turn the inner angle are reflective of the angle of the corner. The two stitches also share a needle hole forming a V shape thereby helping to maintain a sharp corner.

Other general guidelines:

1 Placement of the couching stitch should be perpendicular to the metal thread at the point of couching.

2 Length of the stitch should just hug the threads being couched.

3 Stitch direction generally comes up from the right of the threads and down to the left except for curves where stitches should come up on the inside curve and down on the outside curve.

4 Where second and subsequent rows are stitched to abut previous rows, the couching stitch is worked towards the previous rows. As far as possible, couching should proceed in a clockwise direction as this helps to maintain the twist of the thread. This is, of course, not always possible so watch the thread as you stitch and tighten the twist as necessary. In any event, whenever couching metal threads, attention should always be paid to this aspect to ensure that the twist, and therefore the shine, of the metal thread is maintained.

Yuzen Dyeing

Yuzen dyeing is a technique that became popular towards the end of the 17th century and into the 18th century and revolutionised the decoration for the *kosode* (predecessor of the kimono). It is a paste resist dyeing method with the paste originally derived from different rice products. It is characterised by fine lines and subtle gradation of colours in patterned areas. As a freehand technique, fabric became a blank canvas for the *yuzen* artisan. This facilitated designs that were highly complex, colourful and unique. The process itself is laborious and multi-faceted making it expensive and it is a true Japanese traditional handicraft.

It is very interesting to note that the use of *yuzen* dyeing for decorating *kosode* and later, kimono, is the product of the creativity discussed in this book. It was made famous by a fan artist, Miyazaki Yuzensai, who was much sought after for his intricate and beautiful paintings on folding fans. It was also said that he pioneered *yuzen* dyeing and his designs and *yuzen* dyeing were used to decorate *kosode* of the period.

Additional adornments in the form of gold leaf, goldwork and embroidery were subsequently applied, adding further to the enrichment and beautification of *kosode* and later, kimono. Today, there exists different forms of *yuzen* dyeing with new developments in design and techniques.

Woman's Kimono (Furisode). Japan, Edo period (1615-1868), late 18th-early 19th century.

Kosode (Kimono) Fragment with Wisteria. Japan, Edo period (1615-1868), early 18th century.

This begs the question – can bead embroidery be creatively combined with *yuzen* dyeing? If it has been done with gold leaf, goldwork and embroidery, why not beads? While I have not ventured into learning *yuzen* dyeing, the idea can be borrowed to enhance bead embroidery. Today there are fabric paints that can be used to produce a similar effect. Experimenting has resulted in a few favourite brands that produce a good outcome without altering the fabric hand. They are mixable, so colour range becomes extensive. They can also be diluted and, most importantly, they do not spread when handled appropriately. They can all be heat-set with the iron ensuring longevity of colour.

Here are a few tried and tested brands:

- *Pebeo setacolor* has an opaque range that works well on dark fabrics and is manufactured in France. The colour range is somewhat limited, but colours can be mixed to expand the range.

- For colours with a bit of sparkle, nothing beats *Jacquard Lumiere*. It is from the USA and has a good range of colours that are fully mixable. Have fun with it.

- Japanese brand, *Posca*, is fantastic, especially for fine lines. They come in a pen form with a bullet shaped nib in different thicknesses. If colour is required for painting rather than drawing, allow extra ink to flow onto a palette by holding down the nib. Dip a paint brush and paint as normal.

HINT: *When working with dark silk fabric, diluted metallic colours may be absorbed leaving only the base metallic colour of gold or silver. To prevent this from happening, first work a light layer of pale, non-metallic colour then layer on the colour you like. My favourites for this are Pebeo shimmer opaque and Jacquard Lumiere pearl white.*

Apart from the paint, a few good paint brushes (acrylic are best) in different sizes and a palette (a porcelain one is recommended).

For every project in this section, different creative aspects discussed in this book can be identified. These include:

- Same design—different colourways
- Same design—different techniques
- Same style—different design
- Same design—different interpretation of pattern
- Colour shading with beads

Special points of interest for each project are highlighted. Watch for the atmosphere and underlying ideas within each design and its alternative interpretation.

Before we delve into the projects there are some design elements that are common and apart from the colours or type of beads used, they are stitched using the same technique. These are described below and will not be repeated in the individual projects.

Simple 5-petal flower

Attach a bead at the centre. Attach five beads around the centre. Begin by stitching three beads in place in a 'Y' shape, stitching towards the flower centre. Add the remaining two beads in the large spaces.

Simple multi petal flower— Variation 1

At the flower centre attach a size 11 bead. The petals are worked with a combination of size 11 and size 15 beads.

All petals are stitched towards the flower centre with the larger beads on the outside. Begin by stitching the north-south petals then work the east-west ones. Complete the flower by adding petals between those already worked. Depending on the size of the flower these may be one, two or three petals. Using the needle with the single thread couch between each bead, working as back stitches around the flower.

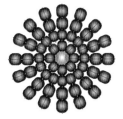

Simple multi petal flower— Variation 2

For the flower centre, stitch a single size 11 bead and encircle this with size 15 beads using *line of held thread—circle method*. The petals are worked in the same manner as Variation 1.

Standard leaves—separated single layer

Commence with stitching the mid-vein with two, three or four (depending on the size and shape of the leaf) beads in the main leaf colour and the required number of size 15 beads to complete the leaf vein with *couching technique 1 — combination needle-koma method*. The first couching stitch starts after the last bead of the main leaf colour. Couch between every bead after that until the end.

Stitch the sides of the leaf with diagonal stitches down both each side of the vein. Begin at the tip and work towards the base. Ensure that the angle of the diagonal stitches flows with the curve of the leaf.

On completion, tie down stitches as necessary to create further shaping for the diagonal stitches.

Line of staggered diagonals with metal thread

Some stems in the projects are stitched with no. 1 metal threads instead of beads using **line of staggered diagonal technique – 3-step method.** The threads are half hitched onto the needle and stitched doubled. Begin with a stitch half the desired stitch length suited for the curve of the stem.

a) Work a second stitch beginning to the immediate right of the first stitch at the same level. This stitch is twice the length of the first stitch and is the full stitch length.

b) The third stitch is the full stitch length and commences halfway up the previous stitch.

c) Repeat step (b) until the end.

d) The final stitch is a half stitch length to complete the sequence.

NOTE: All stitching must be done in such a way that stitch progression follows a clockwise direction.

If tapering is required, omit the half stitch length at the beginning or the end as required.

Straight line

Curved line

THE PROJECTS

PLANNING THE STITCHING AND TECHNIQUE APPLICATION SEQUENCE

The work order in the embroidery is always as follows:

1 Outline for design (if required)

2 Beading design using the following principles.

3 Background

To ensure the best possible aesthetic outcome, preserving the design lines of motifs is desirable coupled, of course, with correct choice and application of techniques. Here are some Japanese embroidery principles for guidance:

- Look initially at the overall design and identify the principal foreground motifs. Work these in order of relative prominence within the overall design. In doing so, the shapes of the design motifs will always be maintained both individually and collectively.

- When working individual motifs, identify the elements within the motif where design lines need to be preserved and work these in sequence of importance within the motif. In doing so, you will achieve maximum visual effect and retain clear design lines.

- Decide on the technique to be applied and commence stitching in the sequence as determined.

These principles and the techniques will be explored further as we apply them to the various projects in this book.

ENCHANTED

A fun piece with simple stitches and cheerful colours – something to create over a weekend perhaps. The same design is also worked in a different colourway with metallic beads and metal threads, showing how a simple change of one variable can set a totally different tone for the project.

The finished wallet measures
8.5cm x 12cm wide (3 ⅜" x 4 ¾").

Techniques Used:

*Couching technique 1 – combination
needle-koma*

Diagonal single layer

Diagonal single layer – metallic thread

Japanese running stitch

Line of held thread – straight line

Line of held thread – curved line

Scatter effect technique – singles

Separated single layer

Simple five-petal flower

Simple multi-petal flower

*Single stitches with one and multiple
beads*

Straight stitch

Vertical single layer

Fabric and supplies

25cm x 18cm wide (10" x 7") piece of
dark brown silk taffeta

18cm x 12cm wide (7" x 4 ¾") piece of
1mm adhesive felt

12-card dark chocolate zipped wallet
frame

50wt off-white cotton sewing thread

50wt dark chocolate brown cotton
sewing thread

50wt sapphire blue cotton sewing
thread

12wt black *Wonderfil* Egyptian cotton
thread

Jacquard Lumiere metallic paint 561 gold

Size 5 acrylic paint brush

Craft glue

Needles

No. 3 milliner's
No. 11 sharp
No. 12 sharp

Beads and thread

*Bead quantities listed refer to a
5cm x 12mm (2" x ½") tube*

CZECH 2mm FIRE-POLISHED BEADS
A = patina copper bronze (3 pieces)

PRECIOSA SIZE 9 3-CUT BEADS
B = red AB (⅛)

PRECIOSA SIZE 12 3-CUT BEADS
C = green lustre (⅔)

TOHO SIZE 8 SEED BEADS
D = 22B silver-lined med topaz
(2 pieces)

TOHO SIZE 11 SEED BEADS
E = 6C transparent amethyst (¾)
F = 10 transparent orange (⅛)
G = 13 transparent lt sapphire (⅛)
H = 22 silver-lined lt topaz (⅛)

I = 174B transparent
rainbow med
orange (¼)
J = 388 inside colour
lt topaz salmon-
lined (¼)
K = 934 inside
colour lt sapphire
opaque purple-
lined (¼)

TOHO SIZE 15 SEED
BEADS
L = 5C transparent ruby (⅛)
M = 6C transparent
amethyst (⅛)
N = 10B transparent med
orange (1/16)
O = 22 silver-lined lt topaz (⅓)
P = 22C silver-lined topaz (1/16)
Q = 25C silver-lined Siam ruby
(20 pieces)
R = 108 transparent lustre peridot (¼)
S = 108B transparent lustre med
peridot (⅛)
T = 388 inside colour lt topaz salmon-
lined (⅛)
U = 928 inside colour rainbow rosaline
opaque purple-lined (1/16)

TOHO SIZE 12 3-CUT BEADS
V = 5B transparent Siam ruby (¼)
W = 103 transparent lustre lt topaz (⅛)
X = 142 Ceylon banana cream
(30 pieces)

SIZE 1 JAPANESE METAL THREAD
Y = lilac

enchanted

DESIGN AND PATTERN PREPARATION

See the liftout pattern for the embroidery design.

Preparing the fabric

On the wrong side, mark the fabric warp with thread or a removable fabric marker.

Transferring the design

Transfer the design referring to page 122.

Mount the fabric on the frame referring to pages 123–125.

Mark the outline with thread using **line of held thread technique** for the straight sections and **Japanese running stitch** for the curved sections.

Gilding the background

Apply the gilding before commencing the embroidery.

1   Gild all petals for the orange flowers. Dilute the paint before applying. Only a light wash is required. Gild the petals down to the sepals on the pointed flowers.

2   Gild all the centres for the group of three flowers positioned in the centre of the design with a light wash.

3   If desired, apply a light wash of gilding to the leaves.

ORDER OF WORK

Round flowers

These flowers are stitched as simple multi-petal flowers with a small variation. Stitch a single bead at the centre of each flower using **A** for the light mauve flower and **D** for the remaining two flowers.

Begin by working the stitches in the north-south direction using 3 x size 11 and 2 x size 15 beads with the larger

beads on the outer edge and leaving a gap at the centre. Work the stitches in the east-west direction then a stitch between each pair in the same manner. The petals are created with stitches of five beads, finishing one bead short of the centre, using the following colours:

Orange flower – 3 x **I**, 2 x **L**
Light mauve flower – 3 x **G**, 2 x **U**
Dark mauve flower – 3 x **K**, 2 x **U**

Complete each flower by working further stitches in the remaining spaces, finishing each stitch one bead short of the centre and using:

Orange flower – 2 x **I**, 1 x **N**, 1 x **L**
Light mauve flower – 2 x **G**, 2 x **U**
Dark mauve flower – 3 x **K**, 1 x **U**

Flower 1

Stitch the two leaves at the base of the flower with **O** for the vein and **R**. Work the simple five-petal flowers with **H** for the centre and

K for the petals. Stitch the stems with **O** using **line of held thread – curved line method**. Work the stamens using random straight stitches in a fan shape to form the filaments using **Y**, half-hitched onto the needle to form a double thread, and single **Q** for the anthers.

Flower 2

Work the calyx with **R** using **diagonal single layer technique** and right diagonal for the left sepal and left

diagonal for the right sepal. Begin at the tip and stitch towards the base. Stitch the fan of gold lines using **line of held thread – curved line method** beginning with the centre line and using **H** tapering to **O** at the tips and **P** at the base. Work the petals, beginning with the foreground petal, forming each one with two stitches using **J** tapering to **T** and **N**. Ensure a neat tip with careful stitch placement. Add a stitch down the centre of each petal with **J** tapering to **T** or only **T** where necessary.

Flower 3

Outline the centre sepal with **R** using two straight stitches to form the tip and working the long sides using **couching technique 1 – combination needle-koma method**. Work a stitch down the centre with 1 x **O**, 3 x **H** and 2 x **P**. Stitch each side sepal with **R** using **diagonal single layer technique** and right diagonal for the left sepal and left diagonal for the right sepal. Begin at the tip and stitch towards the base. Stitch the petals, beginning with the foreground petal, using **vertical single layer technique**. Work the stitch down the centre of the petal first then stitches from side to side with 1 x **F**, 2–3 x **I**, 1–2 x **N** and the number of **L** required for the stitch length. The number of beads is adjusted based on the colour and shape of the petal. Omit **L** from the outermost stitches of each petal.

Red flower

Work a simple five-petal flower using **K** for the centre and **X** for the petals. Stitch the large petals with three stitches using **vertical single layer technique**.

Work the centre stitch with 1 x **L**, 2 x **B** and 3 x **O**. Make a stitch on each side of the centre with 1 x **L**, 2–3 x **B** and 1 x **L**. Ensure a neat tip with careful stitch placement.

Round gold flower

Stitch the flower as a *simple multi-petal flower – variation 1* with an **A** bead for the centre and **O** and **W** for the petals.

Small red flowers

Stitch a single **X** at the base of the flower and add petals with **J** and **T**, using **T** only in the outer petals, or **B** and **L** using **B** only in the outer petals. Work the stems with **O** using *couching technique 1 – combination needle-koma method* for longer lines and *line of held thread – curved line method* for short lines.

Leaves

All the leaves are worked as standard leaves using *separated single layer technique* with the following colours:

Leaves with red veins – **L** and **V** with white thread for veins, **C** with sapphire blue thread.

Leaves with gold veins – **H** and **O** for veins, **C** with white thread.

Small leaves without veins – **R** or **S** using *diagonal single layer technique* beginning at the tip. If the curve from the tip is clockwise use a right diagonal, if counter-clockwise use a left diagonal.

Background

Fill the background using *scatter effect technique – singles* with **E**, taking care to ensure that they are placed approximately 2mm (¹⁄₁₆") apart and face different directions. Change to **M** in tapered and narrow areas.

It is very important that the size of the beaded area is an exact fit to the wallet frame. To ensure this, the background should be stitched in two stages.

1   Begin filling the background from the centre of the design, working out towards the edges. Do not stitch beyond the edge of the flower motifs at this stage.

    Measure the marked outline to ensure that it still measures 11.5cm x 17.5cm wide (4 ½" x 6 ⅞") and adjust if necessary.

2   Complete filling the background right to the edge of the marked area.

CONSTRUCTION

All seam allowances are 1cm (⅜").

1   Complete the finishing process referring to page 132.

2   Using the black pen, transfer the felt template shaping to tracing paper and cut out. Pin the template to the felt and cut out.

3   Place the beaded fabric in the frame, wrong side uppermost, onto a towel over a hard surface. Peel away the backing paper and position the felt, adhesive side down, over the wrong side of the embroidery and press gently. Check to ensure that the felt is positioned correctly. The stitching marking the outline should be visible outside the felt (diag 1).

Apply pressure to the felt in a sweeping motion from the centre outwards to ensure the felt is securely attached. Remove the fabric from the frame. Leaving a 1cm (¾") seam allowance, cut out.

Beginning and ending 2cm (¾")

from one corner, work a line of small running stitches with the off-white sewing thread, 5mm (³⁄₁₆") from the raw edge (diag 2).

Pull up the thread until the fabric gathers neatly behind the corner and secure. Repeat on the remaining corners. Fold under the seam allowance along each straight edge and tack in place using the same thread. The beads at the edge of the design should sit slightly over the folded edge of the fabric.

4   Mark the centre on the upper and lower short edges of the beaded fabric and on both sides of the zip on the wallet frame.

Cut a 40cm (16") length of black *Wonderfil* thread.

Match the marked points of the beaded fabric and zip. Secure the thread at the halfway point into the seam allowance of the beaded fabric close to the marked centre with two back stitches (diag 3).

Beginning at the marked centre point, ladder stitch the beaded fabric to the zip tape, working 3mm (⅛") above the stitched line on the tape. Stitch to 1.5cm (⅝") past the rounded corner and unthread the needle, leaving the excess thread hanging (diag 4).

Return to the starting point and thread the remaining half into the needle. Attach the second half of the fabric to the zip in the same manner, again leaving the remaining thread hanging (diag 5).

Turn the wallet to the second side and attach the second end of the fabric to the zip tape in the same manner.

Re-thread one of the hanging threads and continue attaching the fabric to the zip with ladder stitch, stitching up to the zip teeth then back along the seam for 1cm (⅜") to reinforce the stitching. Secure the thread and trim away any excess. Complete the remaining three sections using the remaining hanging threads in the same manner.

diag 1

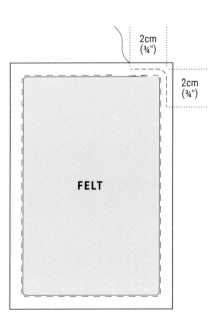

2cm (¾")

2cm (¾")

diag 2

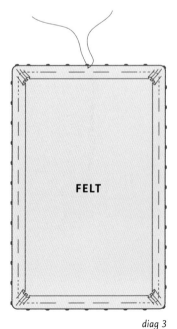

diag 3

5 Gently massage the finished wallet
with your fingers to mould the fit.
Steam the wallet gently and give it a
final moulding with your fingers.

Allow to dry.

1.5cm (⅝")

diag 4

diag 5

JEWELS

This project was designed with overlapping groups of patterns inspired by mandala designs. Mandala patterns lend themselves well to bead embroidery. They are fascinating, possessing the intrinsic characteristics of individual patterns arranged in a harmonious manner into a wider circular shape. This presents not only a circular movement, but the patterns also draw the movement towards the centre core juxtaposed with that which expands outward. Originating in Buddhism, it was Swiss psychiatrist Carl Jung who popularised mandalas in the West, theorising that they represent self and are 'archetypes of wholeness'. He observed that creating mandalas had a calming and focusing effect.

POINTS OF INTEREST

The colour scheme takes on the shades of precious stones and metals – rubies sapphires, emeralds, gold, silver and bronze for a rich display.

Each pattern group presents a distinctive, independent shape within the design creating a mix of rounded and angular motifs.

The design provides challenges of creating linear perspective between the overlapping motifs, at the same time maintaining perspective for the individual pattern groups.

Colour plays an important role in creating overall visual movement. Metallic beads are used in this project – bronze (**H** and **L**) and silver (**Q**).

Group 3 patterns, although a dominant group, are stitched with non-metallic beads and in darker tones to maintain pattern groups and their respective movement.

The finished case measures
7cm x 16.5cm wide (2¾" x 6½").

Techniques Used:

Couching technique 1 – combination needle-koma

Decorative edge

Line of held thread – circle

Line of held thread – curved line

Line of held thread – straight line

Japanese running stitch

Raised effect – general padding

Scatter effect technique – singles

Simple five-petal flower

Single stitches with one or multiple beads

Vertical single layer

Fabric and supplies

20cm x 25cm wide (8" x 10") piece of dark blue silk taffeta

25cm (10") square of black adhesive vinyl

23cm x 13cm wide (9" x 5¼") piece of lightweight fusible interfacing

50wt white cotton sewing thread

50wt dark brown cotton sewing thread

50wt sapphire blue cotton sewing thread

50wt green cotton sewing thread

Metal glasses case frame with hardware and inserts

Multi-use acid-free glue suitable for metal and fabric

5mm (³⁄₁₆") double-sided tape

Needles

No. 10 sharp
No. 12 sharp

Beads

Bead quantities listed refer to a 5cm x 12mm (2" x ½") tube

CZECH 3MM FIRE-POLISHED BEADS
A = emerald (1 piece)
B = gold marbled Siam ruby (3 pieces)

PRECIOSA SIZE 9 3-CUT BEADS
C = ruby lustre (⅔)

PRECIOSA SIZE 12 3-CUT BEADS
D = ruby lustre (¼)

SWAROVSKI MARGUERITE 6MM CRYSTAL
E = crystal shimmer (1 piece)

TOHO SIZE 11 SEED BEADS
F = 241 inside colour rainbow lt topaz mauve-lined (⅛)
G = 551 perma-finish galvanised rose gold (⅛)
H = 594 perma-finish galvanised bronze (¾)

TOHO SIZE 15 SEED BEADS
I = 9B transparent grey (⅛)
J = 13 transparent lt sapphire (¼)
K = 162B transparent rainbow med topaz (20 pieces)
L = 221 bronze (⅓)
M = 241 inside colour rainbow lt topaz mauve-lined (⅛)
N = 457 gold lustre green tea (⅛)
O = 551 perma-finish galvanised rose gold (⅔)
P = 557 perma-finish galvanised starlight (⅛)
Q = 558 perma-finish galvanised aluminium (½)

TOHO SIZE 12 3-CUT BEADS
R = 49 opaque jet (⅔)
S = 82 metallic nebula (¾)
T = 103 transparent lustre lt topaz (⅓)
U = 108 transparent lustre peridot (¼)
V = 355 inside colour crystal Siam-lined (¼)

TOHO SIZE 15 3-CUT BEADS
W = 49 opaque jet (¹⁄₁₆)
X = 82 metallic nebula (½)
Y = 108 transparent lustre peridot (⅛)

DESIGN AND PATTERN PREPARATION

See the liftout pattern for the embroidery design.

Preparing the fabric

On the wrong side, mark the fabric warp with thread or a removable fabric marker.

Transferring the design

Transfer the design referring to page 122. Mount the fabric on the frame referring to pages 123–125. Mark in the outline and darts with thread using *line of held thread technique* for straight sections and *Japanese running stitch* for curved sections.

ORDER OF WORK

The beads are embroidered up to and abut the outline on the outer side except for the darts where the beads are embroidered up to and abut the outline on the inner side.

Pattern group 1

Work line **A** with **H** using *couching technique 1 – combination needle-koma method*. Stitch the main dome outline with two separate lines, beginning on the left-hand side and working from the base to the tip using **H**. Complete the shape with the second line, working from the tip to the base, ensuring a neat point with accurate stitch placement.

Work the motifs inside the domed shape in the following manner:

Stitch a single **B** at the centre of the flower shape and encircle with **U** using *line of held thread – circle method* and green sewing thread. Work pairs of straight stitches alternating four **G** and

H, radiating from the centre, beginning with the pair aligned to the dome tip. Work one side of the shape then the other. Stitch line B in a similar manner to line A with **L**. Outline the four petal shapes in a similar manner to the main dome shape with **H**, adding 3–4 x **L** at the base and 2–3 x **L** at the tip to taper the lines. Fill each petal with fanned stitches with **S** and **X** stitched with black securing thread for the lower group of stitches. Begin with the centre stitch, aligning it with the tip of the petal then work stitches to one side then the other, using **X** at the tips and for the outermost stitches. Work the upper group of fanned stitches in a similar manner using **L** and **O** on the outer edge. End the stitches with a one-point space before the edge of the lower stitches. Adjust the number of **O** so that they make up at least ⅔ of each line.

Fill the background on each leaf shape with *scatter effect technique – singles* using **I** and sapphire blue sewing thread.

Pattern group 2 – part 1

This pattern appears in two places on the design and is completed in two parts during the embroidery process.

Work the curved foundation line of the smaller motif with **H** using *couching technique 1 – combination needle-koma method*.

Pattern group 3 – part 1

This pattern appears in two places on the design and is completed in two parts during the embroidery process.

Work the larger shape at this stage.

Stitching in a clockwise direction, outline the shape with **Q** using *couching technique 1 – combination needle-koma method* for longer lines and *line of held thread – curved line technique* for short lines. Ensure neat points and corners with accurate stitch placement.

Work diagonal stitches that abut the inner line with **V** and **M** where tapering is required, or **V** will not fit, working from

GROUP 1

GROUP 2

GROUP 3

GROUP 4

GROUP 5

GROUP 6

GROUP 7

BACKGROUND
ELEMENTS

LINE B   LINE A

the tip to the base. Fill the background with **scatter effect technique – singles** with I and sapphire blue sewing thread.

Pattern group 4

Use black sewing thread when stitching **S**.

Motif outlines

Beginning with the foreground shape, work the large outline with **C** using *couching technique 1 – combination needle-koma method*, working two lines. Begin stitching on the left-hand side, working from the base to the tip. Work the second line stitching from the tip to the base, ensuring a neat tip with accurate stitch placement. Stitch a second outline in a similar manner inside the first with **S**. Work the inner outline in a similar manner to the large outline with **S**. Stitch the outlines on the two background shapes in the same manner.

Inner shape motif

On the foreground motif, work a straight stitch of 4–5 x **C** tapering to **D** or **M**, if the larger beads will not fit, using *line of held thread – straight line technique*. Couch between each bead. At each end of the line work three stitches, working the centre stitch first with 3 x **Y** and the sapphire blue sewing thread and adding a stitch at a 45 degree angle on each side with 2 x **Y** and the same thread. Repeat on the background motifs, omitting the three stitches at the base. Work four straight stitches with 2 x **Y** along each side of the centre line at a right angle.

Outer shape motifs

Work a *simple five-petal flower* at the marked positions on the foreground shape with **F** for the centre and **T** for the petals. Stitch the V shapes with two stitches of 2–3 x **O**. Add a single **L** inside each V shape aligned vertically to the point.

On the background shapes work diagonal stitches abutting the inner shape with 2 x **F** for each stitch, tapering with **M** where necessary.

Fill the background on each shape using s*catter effect technique – singles* with J and sapphire blue sewing thread.

Pattern group 5

The pattern consists of four overlapping elements. Working from foreground to background, stitch the double border on each element with **Q** using *couching technique 1 – combination needle-koma method*, ensuring neat corners with accurate stitch placement.

Within each double outline, stitch single beads alternating **C** and **X**, spaced slightly apart and aligned perpendicular to the inner outline.

Work the flower within the foreground element, beginning with a single **X** at the centre and encircling with **Q** using *line of held thread – circle method*. Work radiating stitches with 2 x **P** around the circle, beginning with stitches at the cardinal points and finishing each stitch one bead space from the circle. Add two radiating stitches between each cardinal point using the same beads, aligning each stitch to the centre.

Work fanned straight stitches within the centre elements, beginning with a stitch with 4 x **C**. Add a single stitch on each side of the centre with 3 x **C** and add two stitches on each side of the previous three stitches, the first with 2 x **O** and the second with 1 x **O**.

Outline the semi-circle within the background element with **G** using *line of held thread – curved line method*. Work a second outline inside the first with **O**. Stitch the single **A** at the centre of the semi-circle, aligning the bead to the inward point. Work fanned stitches around the semi-circle beginning with the centre stitch with 4 x **C**, then 3 x **C** on each side, 2 x **O** on each side and finish with two stitches with 4 x **V** on each side.

Fill the background of each element using *scatter effect technique – singles* with **I** and sapphire blue sewing thread.

Pattern group 2 – part 2

Work the curved foundation line of the large motif with **H** using *couching technique 1 – combination needle-koma method*. Stitch each small leaf shape with two stitches, beginning with the foreground shape and working each stitch with **O** using *line of held thread – curved line method*. Continue stitching the shapes from foreground to background, ensuring neat points with accurate stitch placement. Repeat on the smaller motif. Work a vein line along the centre of each shape on both motifs with **S**, tapering at each end with **X**, using the black sewing thread and *line of held thread – curved line method*.

Pattern group 3 – part 2

Complete the smaller shape in the same manner as the larger shape.

Pattern group 6

Attach **E** with **J** at the centre of the flower and surround with **Q** using *couching technique 1 – combination needle-koma method*. After couching the first bead, couch every second bead. At the end of the circle, take the needle through the first bead. Complete the couching between the beads, shaping the circle further.

Stitch the outer circle with **O** in the same manner as the centre circle. Add spaced single stitches on the inner edge of the outer circle with **T**, aligning the beads at a right-angle to the outer circle. Work a decorative edge around the circle with **X** using the circle to guide stitch placement. Adjust the number of beads as required.

Stitch the scalloped edge of the pattern with **O**, working each scallop separately using *couching technique 1 – combination needle-koma method*. Work a second scalloped line inside the first with **S**.

Stitch the central flower petals, beginning with any petal then stitching alternate petals until the flower is complete, in the following manner:

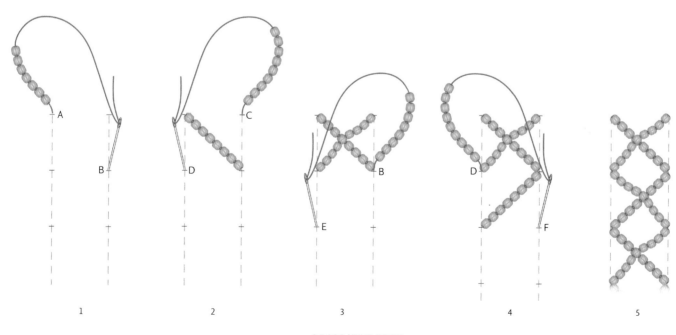

1   2   3   4   5

DECORATIVE EDGE

Using **raised effect – general padding**, work a stitch with 4 x **M** across the centre of the petal, leaving a one bead space between the ends of the stitch and the edge of the petal. Stitch the petal with five stitches using **vertical single layer technique** with **C** and **D**, placing **C** on the outer edge and adjusting the number of beads to suit the length of the stitch and to taper. Work the centre stitch first then alternate from side to side, pin stitching after each stitch.

Work the circle of **simple five-petal flowers** with **M** for the centre and **Q** for the petals.

Stitch the small patterns at the base of each scallop with three stitches, beginning with the centre stitch with 2 x **U** and 1 x **O**. Add an angled stitch on each side with 2 x **U**. Fill the background using **scatter effect technique – singles** with **J** and the sapphire blue sewing thread.

Pattern group 7

This pattern appears in two places on the design with a variation at the tip.

Outline the pattern using **couching technique 1 – combination needle-koma method**, beginning with **L** at the tip and changing to **H** when the pattern widens.

Tip variation 1

Work a straight stitch with 1 x **B**, 1 x **U** and 1 x **L**, aligning the stitch to the outline. Work fanned stitches around the stitch, beginning at the centre then working the stitches on one side then the other with **O**, **G** and **L** for the centre stitch and **O** and **L** for the other stitches. Place **O** on the outer edge of all stitches.

Tip variation 2

Work a semi-circle line with **P** using **couching technique 1 – combination needle-koma method**. Add a single **B** at the centre of the semi-circle and work spaced single stitches with 1 x **T** around the edge of the semi-circle, placing them at right-angles to the shape.

Background elements

Paisley shape – Outline the shape with **N** using **couching technique 1 – combination needle-koma method**. Add single **G** and **O** with **G** in the wider section.

Large flowers – Stitch a single **W** at the centre and encircle with **Q** using **line of held thread – circle technique**. Work radiating stitches with 2 x **P** around the circle, beginning with stitches at the cardinal points and finishing each stitch one bead space from the circle. Add two radiating stitches between each cardinal point using the same beads, aligning each stitch to the centre.

Medium flowers – Stitch a single **F** at the centre of the flower. Work each petal radiating out from the centre with 1 x **T** and **K** beginning with the north and south stitches. Work two, evenly spaced stitches in each half.

Small flowers – Stitch as **simple five-petal flowers** using **F** for the centre and **T** or **Q** for the petals.

Background

Fill the remaining background area using **scatter effect technique – singles** with **R** and **W** and black sewing thread, using **W** in small spaces.

CONSTRUCTION

The glasses case comprises two sections – an upper section to which the beaded fabric is attached and a lower section that is covered with adhesive vinyl.

All seam allowances are 2cm (¾") unless specified.

Upper section

1   Complete the finishing process referring to page 132.

2   Using the template, cut out the fusible interfacing. With the beading still on the frame, position and fuse the interfacing to the back of the beaded fabric.

3   Remove the beaded fabric from the frame and cut out leaving a 2cm (¾") seam allowance. Stitch the darts with ladder stitch and trim away any excess fabric.

4   Place double-sided tape lengthwise and crosswise on the case. Centre the beaded piece over the case and press in position.

5   Apply a thin layer of glue around the flat edge of the case and press the beaded fabric in place. The edge of the beading should fit exactly to the edge of the case. Allow to dry.

6   Trim the seam allowance to 1cm (⅜").

Apply a thin layer of glue to the inside flat edge of the case. Fold over the seam allowance and press in place. Allow to dry.

Lower section

1   Place the interfacing template along the bias of the adhesive vinyl. Leaving a 1.5cm (⅝") seam allowance, cut out.

2   Peel away the paper backing and centre the vinyl over the case and press into position, smoothing the surface. At each corner, pull the vinyl firmly to smooth out the excess.

3   Using a hairdryer, carefully heat one corner and while warm, pull the vinyl to smooth out any remaining wrinkles. Repeat on the remaining corners.

4   Trim the seam allowance to 1cm (⅜") and fold over the edge of the case. Trim the seam allowance to reveal the metal prongs and press firmly in place.

Assembling the case

1   Remove the two clips holding the hinge rigid.

2   Slip one side of the hinge into the metal prongs on the case. Bend and press the prongs down to secure. Repeat on the second half of the case.

3   Apply a thin layer of glue to the inside of the case. Position the case lining and press firmly in place. Allow to dry.

A DIFFERENT INTERPRETATION

Spectacle Case – Jewels by Sue Fox

Sue Fox stitched the alternative project. She chose her own colour scheme and I had, as with all the others, deliberately withheld my own thoughts on the design. Note where Sue made some alterations to some parts of the pattern to make the design a better fit for her colour scheme.

"My journey started nearly 10 years ago when I saw a class advertised in our Embroiderers' Guild, Victoria newsletter. "Aha," said I, "that sounds like fun, I love beads, I'll go to that." Until then I had never heard of Japanese bead embroidery, or of tutor Margaret Lee, but I registered,

and took myself off to the Guild in Melbourne for a two-day class.

No-one warned me about size 12 needles or size 15 beads, or the exacting standard of work that Margaret sets for all her students. The fact that I was just about due for cataract surgery didn't exactly help either.

By halfway through day one, I was ready to burst into tears and give up; I couldn't thread the needles, couldn't stitch the right beads in the right places, and it was an absolute disaster!

To this day I still don't know why I kept on going, or how I became totally and completely hooked, doing more two-day classes at the Guild, then joining Margaret's regular private classes in Melbourne, and have kept on coming

back for class after class through all these years.

But I am so glad I did!

There is just something about the beauty and simplicity of the Japanese approach to design and colour, combined with the lustre and texture of beads in all shapes, sizes and colours, that really speaks to my creative spirit.

So, my advice to anyone is 'If you are struggling, don't give up too soon! It will all fall into place before long if you just keep persevering.'

With much help and support from Margaret I have gradually improved my skill in designing my own work, and I felt very honoured when Margaret asked me to contribute a piece to this book.

From a choice of different projects, I opted for the glasses case because I saw immediately that I could put my own stamp on it, while still adhering to the design and structure principles of Japanese bead embroidery. We began with a simple line drawing, and because they are my favourite colours, naturally I chose blues, greens and turquoises with silver and bronze to lift and highlight them. Margaret put a selection of beads together, and away I went, firstly colouring in to get a rough design plan, then some stitching, plenty of unpicking and re-doing. There was one change of plan along the way and the only difficulty was making sure that my proposed change would not affect the overall integrity of the design or deviate from the set protocols. As it turned out, I simply used a different stitch and a lighter shade of bead and came up with something that had much more light and movement than what I had originally intended to do. I had lots of encouragement and input from Margaret along the way, and now finally it has all come together.

I have really enjoyed this project, despite the pressure to keep my work at the highest possible standard (which isn't always quite as high as I'd like it to be!) and I hope that it will inspire others to express their own individuality. Once you understand the design protocols involved, and how to make small changes that don't affect the integrity of the work, you can use the colours that you are comfortable with and allow them to inspire you and make your work your own, not a carbon copy of someone else's.

And last but far from least, my thanks to Margaret, who has patiently led me on this long journey, filled my head with knowledge and my soul with joy, and enriched my life more than she will ever know."

SHIPPO FLOWERS

This design is inspired by a *wagara* pattern, *shippo*. *Wagaras* are traditional Japanese patterns passed down through generations and are steeped in tradition and meaning. The *shippo* pattern can be traced back to the 8th century and is created by circles overlapping in quarters, resulting in shapes that resemble petals. The petals align in a 45-degree lattice and produce a centre in the form of a four-pointed star.

The *shippo* is regarded as auspicious and symbolises prosperity, bonds of good relationship and the unending and expanding chain of harmony and peace. It also represents the seven treasures of Buddhism (gold, silver, lapis lazuli, agate, pearl, coral, and crystal) each of which represents a mental quality valued as part of Buddhist practice-mindfulness, investigation, energy, joy, tranquillity, concentration, and equanimity.

The *shippo* is an interesting pattern. It always stirs in me the feeling of something deeper beyond the basic image. In this design, *Shippo Flowers*, the *shippo* shape is expanded to incorporate an eight-pointed flower linked by a secondary pattern. While I see interesting shapes emerging in the pattern, I was interested to see how it will be viewed by others as it presents many creative possibilities.

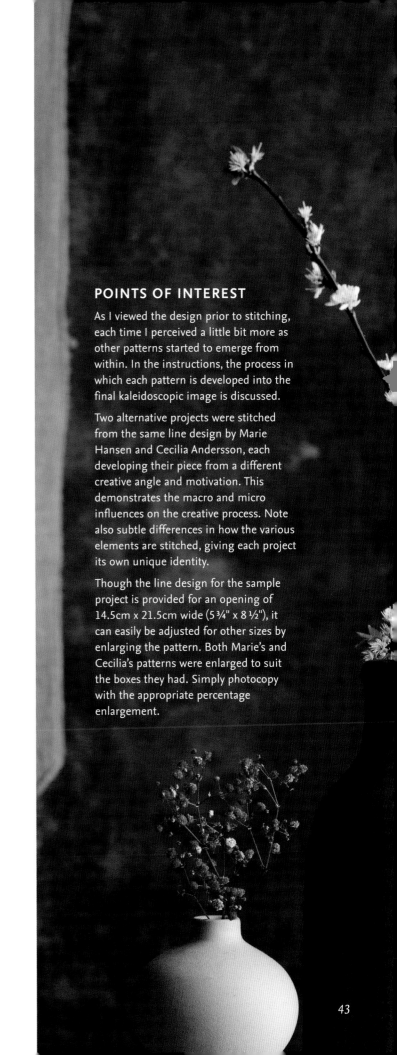

POINTS OF INTEREST

As I viewed the design prior to stitching, each time I perceived a little bit more as other patterns started to emerge from within. In the instructions, the process in which each pattern is developed into the final kaleidoscopic image is discussed.

Two alternative projects were stitched from the same line design by Marie Hansen and Cecilia Andersson, each developing their piece from a different creative angle and motivation. This demonstrates the macro and micro influences on the creative process. Note also subtle differences in how the various elements are stitched, giving each project its own unique identity.

Though the line design for the sample project is provided for an opening of 14.5cm x 21.5cm wide (5¾" x 8½"), it can easily be adjusted for other sizes by enlarging the pattern. Both Marie's and Cecilia's patterns were enlarged to suit the boxes they had. Simply photocopy with the appropriate percentage enlargement.

The finished panel measures
14.5cm x 21.5cm wide (5 ¾" x 8 ½").

Techniques Used:

Line of held thread – curved line

Line of held thread – straight line

Raised effect – stitch length adjustment

Scatter effect technique – singles

Single stitches with one and multiple beads

Straight stitch – metallic thread

Fabric and supplies

25cm x 34cm wide (10" x 13 ½") piece of walnut brown silk taffeta

17cm x 24cm wide (6 ¾" x 9 ½") piece of medium-weight fusible interfacing

50wt white cotton sewing thread

50wt dark brown cotton sewing thread

Box with 14.5cm x 21.5cm wide (5 ¾" x 8 ½") opening

Needles

No. 11 sharp
No. 12 sharp

Beads and thread

Bead quantities listed refer to a 5cm x 12mm (2" x ½") tube

CZECH 3mm FIRE-POLISHED BEADS
A = saturated metallic kale (24 pieces)

TOHO SIZE 8 SEED BEADS
B = 22 silver-lined lt topaz (1)
C = 557 perma-finish galvanised starlight (35 pieces)

TOHO SIZE 11 SEED BEADS
D = 996 gold-lined rainbow peridot (1)

TOHO SIZE 15 SEED BEADS
E = 9B transparent grey (1)
F = 22 silver-lined lt topaz (⅓)
G = 108 transparent lustre peridot (¾)
H = 329 gold lustre African sunset (¾)
I = 388 inside colour lt topaz salmon-lined (¾)
J = 996 gold-lined rainbow peridot (1¼)

TOHO SIZE 11 HEXAGON BEADS
K = 34 silver-lined smoky topaz (1)

TOHO 3mm BUGLE BEADS
L = 5 transparent lt Siam ruby (1)

METALLIC SEWING THREAD
M = vy lt gold

DESIGN AND PATTERN PREPARATION

See the liftout pattern for the embroidery design.

Preparing the fabric

On the wrong side, mark the fabric warp with thread or a removable fabric marker.

Transferring the design

Transfer the design referring to page 122. Mount the fabric on the frame referring to pages 123–125. Mark in the outline with thread using **line of held thread technique**.

ORDER OF WORK

At each point that the 45 degree grid lines intersect two basic patterns are created. This results in alternating rows of evenly spaced pattern. Stitch these first as they establish the framework required to create the primary *shippo* shapes. Use **M** and the no. 11 sharp to attach the beads, knotting the ends of the thread together to create a double thread.

Intersection A

The pattern here is developed within the design to become the centre of the eight-petal flower pattern that is referred to as pattern 1.

Stitch a single **A** in a vertical direction at the centre of each eight-petal flower.

Work radiating stitches around the centre with **K**, beginning at the cardinal points. Complete with a single stitch in each quarter.

Intersection B

The pattern here begins with a cross and develops into a larger, independent pattern within the design and is referred to as pattern 2.

Stitch a single **C** at the centre of each four-petal flower. Work two **L**, side by side, at each cardinal point.

Creating the *shippo* pattern

Use **M** and the no. 11 sharp to attach the beads, knotting the ends of the thread together to create a double thread.

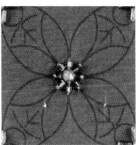

intersection A

intersection B

On pattern 1, bring the needle to the front between the centre bead and one adjoining **K** at a cardinal point. Take the needle through the **K** and pick up 1 x **B**, 1 x **J**, 6 x **D** and 6 x **J**. Take the needle through one bugle bead (**L**) at the centre of pattern 2 and down through the fabric to complete the stitch. Tie down the line of beads using *line of held thread – curved line method*.

Pull gently to tension the stitch and pin stitch to secure. Repeat on all similar lines to complete the *shippo* pattern.

---

*NOTE: When an adjacent line is already in place, the needle comes to the surface between the centre bead and **K** then goes through the **K**, **B** and **J** that are in place, then pick up 6 x **D** and 6 x **J** to complete the stitch.*

Eight-petal flower

Use **M** and the no. 11 sharp to attach the beads, knotting the ends of the thread together to create a double thread.

On pattern 1 bring the needle to the front between the centre bead and adjoining **K**. Take the needle through the **K** and pick up 1 x **D** and 9 x **J**. Take the needle to the back at the end of the design line, ensuring it is positioned to form a point with the first **J** in the outer line.

Adjust the number of beads if necessary to fit the space. Bring the needle to the surface in line ready for a pin stitch but do not work it at this stage. Tie down the line of beads using *line of held thread – curved line method*. Pull gently to tension the stitch and work the pin stitch to secure. Repeat on all similar lines to create the eight-petal flower.

---

*NOTE: When an adjacent line is already in place, the needle comes to the surface between the centre bead and **K** then goes through the **K**, **D** and **J** that are in place, then pick up 8 x **J** to complete the stitch.*

Petal filling

Stitch a single **H** near the tip aligned to the centre bead. Bring the needle to the surface next to **H**, take it through the bead and work a straight stitch to the centre bead. Work one stitch on one side and two stitches on the other side of the first stitch in the same manner, varying the side on which the two stitches are worked.

Design development

At this stage an integrated pattern incorporating three individual patterns has been created: the larger *shippo* pattern, an eight-petal flower and a four-petal flower between the *shippo* shapes. Pattern 1 can also be considered a fourth as it is a simple flower pattern in its own right.

Developing pattern 2 – part 1

Use white cotton sewing thread.

Stitch a curved line between the arms of each cross with **G** using *line of held thread – curved line method*. Fill the curved shape with three stitches with **G**, working the centre stitch with *raised effect – stitch length adjustment technique*, adding one extra bead. Work the side stitches with 2 x **G**, fanning out from the last bead of the first stitch.

shippo flowers

petal lines and the enhanced cross pattern to form an extended squared pattern with outwardly curved points. A contrasting colour is deliberately selected to bring out the pattern.

Completing the design

Fill the background areas between the *shippo* shapes using **scatter effect technique – singles** with **E** and dark brown cotton sewing thread.

CONSTRUCTION

All seam allowances are 2cm (¾").

1   Once the embroidery is complete check the measurements to ensure they are correct for the box size. Adjust if necessary.

2   Complete the finishing process referring to page 132.

3   Measure the box opening and cut out the medium-weight fusible interfacing to an exact fit.

4   Place a towel beneath the beaded surface and fuse the interfacing in place on the wrong side of the beaded panel.

5   Remove the beaded fabric from the frame and cut out leaving a 5cm (2") seam allowance on the short sides and a 6cm (2 ⅜") on the long sides. Lace the beaded fabric over the cardboard backing, checking to ensure it is a neat fit to the box opening.

NOTE: If the box used does not come with cardboard backing, measure the opening and cut a backing from acid-free mat board. If the box does not come with a built-in backing, cut a second piece of mat board to conceal the lacing.

---

6   Place the backing over the wrong side of the laced fabric and fit into the box.

Design development

The integrated pattern now created serves the following purpose.

a   The cross has now been altered into a square, incorporating the cross.

b   The raised stitches bring them to prominence, and they realign the movement back to the 45 degree gridlines of the *shippo* pattern.

Developing pattern 2 – part 2

Use white cotton sewing thread.

Work a single stitch with 4 x **I** and 1 x **F**, aligned with the centre stitch worked in part 1. **F** is positioned adjacent to the curved line.

Add a stitch on each side with 3 x **I**, aligning the tip of each stitch with the tip of a petal on the eight-petal flower. Add two stitches with 2 x **I** between the previous stitches.

Design development

The addition of the last element incorporated the *shippo* pattern, flower

A DIFFERENT INTERPRETATION

Shippo Flowers is also stitched by Marie Hansen and Cecilia Andersson. The boxes they used are a different size to the sample project. The line drawing was adjusted to suit their boxes. Note that the design was also orientated at a different angle for Marie's piece.

The inspiration for their colour schemes was different and their interpretation of the design also varies.

Here is how Marie's colour scheme came about.

> *"The shippo design featured on the top of this jewellery box is a very well recognised symbol in Japanese culture. It is featured on fabrics, embroidery designs in art, on kimono and obi and in paintings.*
>
> *The shippo or tsunagi is an infinitely repeating circular design representing the Seven Jewels or Treasures from the Buddhist Sutras.*
>
> *Stitching with Japanese beads is always a pleasure; the quality, colour and shine always makes the finished project a joy to the eye.*
>
> *The selection of colours came from a piece of fabric lace in my cupboard. I often look at colours in fabric as they are always well coordinated."*

Cecilia's project is a special gift for her beloved granddaughter who loves flowers and whose favourite colours are pink and purple. To maintain a fresh and youthful feel, a silver obi fabric was selected along with other pastel shades of beads to complement the pink and purple. The result is a project developed at the micro level with the five 'Ws'.

NOSHI

The *noshi* is a unique formal
Japanese decorative tradition and is
believed to be a custom dating back
to the twelfth century. *Noshi* were
originally bundles of abalone strips
that had been dried and stretched
thin. They are attached to gifts as
an expression of good wishes to
the recipient. *Noshi* designs are
typically depicted in a bundle tied
together and with uneven ends.
In this design, typical Japanese
patterns decorate the strips. These
patterns include *wagaras* which are
traditional Japanese patterns passed
down through generations. They
are often steeped in symbolism
with meanings important in
Japanese culture.

The folio was stitched by
Frances Langenberg.

Kikko. The *kikko* is an auspicious *wagara* pattern in Japanese design. It is patterned after the shell of the tortoise and a symbol of longevity and intellect. Used initially to decorate court garments, it was later adapted for use in warrior garments, weapons and armour in the samurai age.

The *kikko* pattern used in this design is combined with a flower centre. This combined pattern is referred to as *kikko hanabishi*.

Seigaiha (blue ocean waves). As a country of islands, the ocean is very important to Japan. Many different wave patterns have featured in Japanese textiles. The *seigaiha* is one of them and is made up of a layered pattern of circular arches, representing ocean waves. This *wagara* has been in use since the 16th century and in Japanese embroidery, the pattern decorates both obi and kimono.

Flowing water. Japan is also a country of many streams and rivers, and they symbolise the flow of life and continuity. Flowing water patterns evoke a sense of coolness and are often combined with other patterns to depict different seasons of the year. In this design, flowing water is combined with maple leaves to decorate one of the *noshi* strips.

Tatewaku (Steam Rising). This pattern is held as an auspicious symbol and is traditionally associated with the nobility. Dating back to the *Heian* period (794 to 1185), the pattern is made up of two or more curving lines of alternating symmetrical distension and depressions representing steam gently rising. It has the symbolic suggestion of 'rising above'.

Kiku (Chrysanthemum), is a symbol that represents regal beauty, longevity, and rejuvenation. The sixteen-petal chrysanthemum pattern is the emblem of the Imperial family of Japan.

Higaki (Cypress fence). This pattern is based on a type of fence that uses the bark of the cypress tree, woven into a net pattern.

POINTS OF INTEREST

Note the simultaneity of contrast and balance between the movement of the geometric and curved patterns of the different elements.

The design is stitched as two different projects incorporating Japanese silk embroidery, goldwork and bead embroidery. As the two projects were for different end purposes, the design was stitched in different colour schemes.

Note that techniques and even some of the patterns were altered to suit the project and their ultimate personal purpose.

Instructions are provided for the project stitched by Frances Langenberg who elected to make her embroidery into a folio.

noshi

The finished folio measures
23cm x 32cm wide (9" x 12⅝").

Techniques Used:

Couching pairs technique – metallic thread

Couching pairs – round and round

*Couching technique 1 – combination
needle-koma*

*Diagonal single layer technique – metallic
thread*

Fuzzy effect – metallic thread

Line of held thread – curved line

Line of held thread – straight line

*Line of staggered diagonals – metallic
thread*

Scatter effect technique – singles

Simple multi-petal flower

Single stitches with one and multiple beads

Fabric and supplies

102cm x 70cm wide (40¼" x 27½")
piece of indigo textured silk

66cm x 33cm wide (26" x 13") piece
of 1mm adhesive felt

20cm x 33cm wide (8" x 13") piece
of heavyweight fusible interlining

66cm x 33cm wide (26" x 13") piece of
medium-weight fusible interfacing

50wt off-white cotton sewing thread

50wt black cotton sewing thread

Silver couching thread

2mm x 1.5cm (⅝") neodymium
magnets (3)

2mm x 1cm (⅜") neodymium
magnets (3)

Craft glue

E6000 industrial-strength adhesive

White fabric marker

Needles

No. 24 chenille
No. 3 milliner's
No. 7 sharp
No. 10 sharp
No. 12 sharp

Beads and threads

*Bead quantities listed refer to a
5cm x 12mm (2" x ½") tube*

TOHO SIZE 11 SEED BEADS
A = 1 transparent crystal (¼)
B = 162 transparent rainbow lt topaz
(¼)
C = 241 inside colour rainbow lt topaz
mauve-lined (¾)
D = 457 gold lustre green tea (¼)

TOHO SIZE 15 SEED BEADS
E = 1 transparent crystal (¼)
F = 162 transparent rainbow lt topaz
(¼)
G = 241 inside colour rainbow lt topaz
mauve-lined (⅔)
H = 457 gold lustre green tea (¼)
I = 551 perma-finish galvanised rose
gold (¼)
J = 557 perma-finish galvanised
starlight (1)

TOHO SIZE 12 3-CUT BEADS
K = 557 perma-finish galvanised
starlight (½)

TOHO 3mm BUGLE BEADS
L = 21 silver-lined crystal (1)
M = 22 silver-lined lt topaz (1)
N = 82 metallic nebula (1½)
O = 176 transparent rainbow black
diamond (1)

TOHO SIZE 15 2-CUT BEADS
P = 21 silver-lined crystal (⅓)
Q = 22 silver-lined lt topaz (⅓)

SIZE 1 JAPANESE METAL THREAD
R = gold
S = multi-colour gold
T = silver

SIZE 5 JAPANESE METAL THREAD
U = silver

DESIGN AND PATTERN PREPARATION

See the liftout pattern for the embroidery design.

Preparing the fabric

Cut one, 65cm x 35cm wide (25½" x 14") and one, 102cm x 35cm wide (40¼" x 14") from the indigo silk. On the wrong side, mark the fabric warp with thread or a removable fabric marker. Put the larger piece aside for the lining.

Transferring the design

Transfer the design referring to page 122, positioning the border outline 3.5cm (1⅜") from one short end. Mount the fabric on the frame referring to pages 123–125. Mark in the outline with thread using **line of held thread technique**.

ORDER OF WORK

Preparing the size 5 Japanese metal thread (U)

Measure the length of **U** and cut in half. Following the instructions provided, wind each length of **U** onto one koma.

Ribbon

Outline

Outline the ribbon sections with **U** using **couching pairs – round and round technique**, stitching only one row. This outline serves as padding for subsequent overstitching. Overstitch with **S** using **diagonal single layer technique** working in a right diagonal and clockwise direction. Work the segments from foreground to background.

Inner sections

Fill each section with **U** using **couching pairs – round and round technique**. Begin in a corner and work in a clockwise direction.

Preparing a sinking needle

- Thread a 15cm (6") length of silk thread into a no. 24 chenille needle (diag 1).

- Bring the ends of the thread together and twist the lengths together into a single thread (diag 2).

- Run your fingers along the thread with a light coating of glue and leave to dry.

- Trim any loose threads from the end and thread it through the needle, creating a lasso (diag 3).

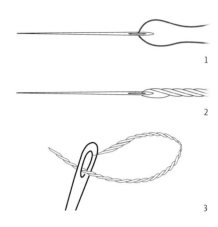

Noshi strips

Outline

Outline each strip in the listed order:

1 *KIKKO* STRIP

Begin the first outline with **O** using **couching technique 1 – combination needle-koma method**. Add a second outline outside the first with **U** using **couching – pairs technique**.

2 *SEIGAIHA* STRIP

Outline the foreground section in a similar manner to the *kikko* strip with **M** and **U**. Outline the background section with three rows of **U** using **couching – pairs technique**. Once the initial pair has been couched, add a single row, couching over it and the adjacent row of the pair in a brick pattern.

3 FLOWING WATER WITH MAPLE LEAVES AND *TATEWAKU* STRIPS

Outline both strips with three rows of **U** in the same manner as the *Seigaiha* background section.

4 *HIGAKI* STRIP

Work the foreground section then the background section. Outline

each section with three rows of **U** in the same manner as the *Seigaiha* background section.

5 FUZZY EFFECT STRIP

Outline with three rows of **U** in the same manner as the *Seigaiha* background section.

Filling patterns

1 *KIKKO*

Begin by establishing the *kikko* pattern. Stitch a line with **L** using **line of held thread – straight line technique** between individual *kikko* outlines, using **P** in spaces too small for a bugle bead.

Add a line on each side with **M** using **line of held thread – straight line technique**, and **Q** in small spaces.

Stitch the inner line with **U** in the no. 24 chenille needle using **line of held thread – straight line technique**.

Stitch a **simple multi-petal flower** in each shape with **K** for the centre and **C** and **G** for the petals, positioning **C** on the outer edge and leaving a one bead space between the centre and petals.

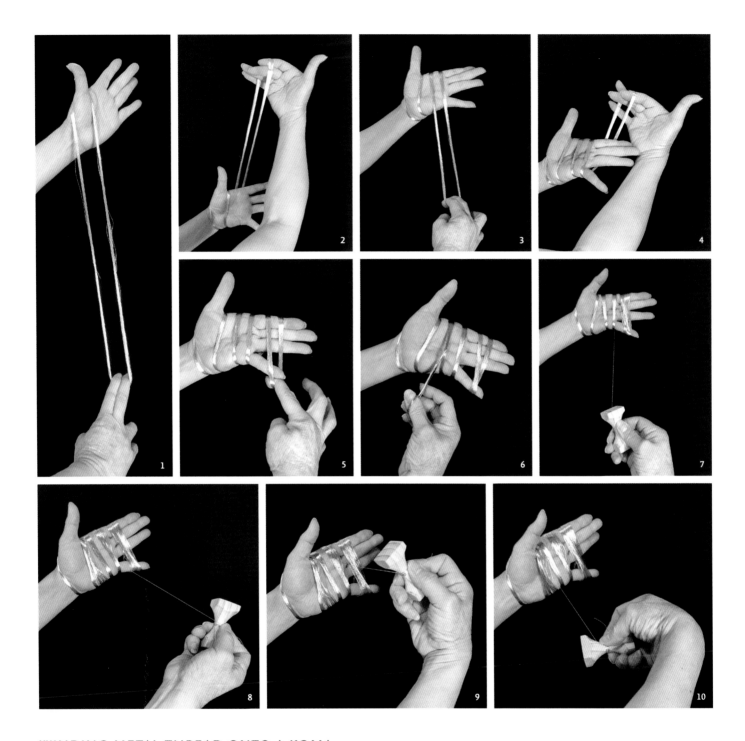

WINDING METAL THREAD ONTO A KOMA

1   Open out the skein and apply tension. Place one end of the loop (not the tied end) over thumb.

2–4   Keeping the thread under tension, bring the skein around the hand twice.

5   Anchor the remaining end of the loop on the fourth or little finger.

6   Release the tied end.

7   Hold the end of the thread onto the koma.

8–10   Wind the koma in a counter-clockwise direction.

2 FLOWING WATER WITH MAPLE LEAVES

Work the water lines first and stitch with **S** using *line of staggered diagonals technique* in a clockwise direction. Stitch the leaves with **I** using *couching technique 1 – combination needle-koma method* for the longer lines and *line of held thread – curved line technique* for short lines.

Ensure neat points with accurate stitch placement.

3 *SEIGAIHA*

Stitch each group of waves in different colours. There are no specific rules regarding colour placement except that the same colour should be used in one group. Begin with the foreground groups and work to the background, working the outermost line with size 11 beads and all other lines with size 15 beads. Stitch the outermost line first then work inwards using *couching technique 1 – combination needle-koma method* for longer lines and *line of held thread – curved line method* for short lines. Use the following colour combinations:

White waves – **A** and **E**
Red waves – **C** and **G**
Yellow waves – **B** and **F**
Green waves – **D** and **H**

4 *TATEWAKU*

Work the curving lines with **L** using *couching technique 1 – combination needle-koma method*. Use **P** in small spaces.

Add random single stitches along the curving lines using **P**, reducing the density towards the top.

5 *HIGAKI*

Stitch each line with bugle beads using *line of held thread – straight line technique*. Where a space is too

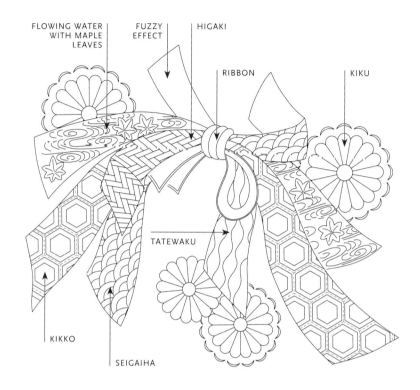

PATTERN GUIDE

small use a 2-cut bead. Use **M** and **Q** for the foreground section and **L** and **P** for the background section.

6 FUZZY EFFECT

Work with **T**, half-hitched onto the no. 7 sharp to form a double thread, using *fuzzy effect technique – metallic thread*. Lines are worked 2mm (¹⁄₁₆") apart and tied down with the silver couching thread.

7 SCATTER EFFECT

Fill the section with **M** using *scatter effect technique – singles*.

8 *KIKU*

There are two parts to the pattern: the flower and the surrounding crescent shapes.

Begin with the crescent shapes, working with **S**, half-hitched onto the no. 7 sharp to form a double thread,

using *diagonal single layer technique*. Use right diagonal and stitch in a clockwise direction.

Work the flower centre with **J** using *couching technique 1 – combination needle-koma method*. Begin the petals with one that abuts the *noshi* strip and work from foreground to background with **K** and **J** using *couching technique 1 – combination needle-koma method* and placing **K** in the curved section above where the petals overlap.

Border

Work the inner edge of the band with two rows of **N** using *line of held thread – straight line technique*. Stitch the outer edge of the band with three rows of **N** in the same manner.

Fill the band with **N** using *scatter effect technique – singles*. This band forms the closing edge of the folio.

CONSTRUCTION

All seam allowances are 1.5cm (⅝")
unless specified

1   Complete the finishing process
referring to page 132.

2   Mark out all the outer edges of the
pattern as indicated on the liftout
pattern with the white fabric marker.
Mark on the wrong side of the fabric
also.

3   Cut the piece of adhesive felt to
measure 59.5cm x 32cm wide (23½"
x 12⅝") to back the beaded piece.

Cut the piece of medium-weight
fusible interfacing to measure 59.3cm
x 31.6cm wide (23⅜" x 12½") for the
lining.

Cut the piece of heavyweight fusible
interlining to measure 31.6cm x
19cm wide (12½" x 7½") for the flap.

BEADED FABRIC

4   Place the beaded fabric on the frame,
wrong side uppermost, onto a towel
over a hard surface. Peel away the
backing and position the felt, adhesive
side down over the wrong side of the
embroidery and press gently. Check
to ensure that the felt is positioned
correctly. The outer edge markings
should be visible outside the felt. Apply
pressure to the felt in a sweeping
motion from the centre outwards to
ensure it is securely attached. Remove

the fabric from the frame and cut out
leaving a 1.5cm (⅝") seam allowance.
Mitre the corners. With the wrong side
uppermost, apply a thin layer of craft
glue to the edge of the seam allowance
only. Fold in the seam allowance and
glue in position. At 1cm (⅜") to the
right of the 46cm (18⅛") mark, place
one 1.5cm (⅝") magnet at the centre
and one on each outer edge and glue
in position with the *E6000* glue.

LINING

5   The lining is a mirror-image of the
beaded fabric. Ensure this position is
maintained while preparing the lining.

Measure and mark a line down the
wrong side of the fabric 62cm (24½")
from the right-hand short edge.

With one edge of the medium-weight
fusible interfacing aligned 2cm (¾")
from the right-hand short edge, fuse
the interfacing to the wrong side of
the fabric lining (diag 1).

Fuse the heavyweight fusible
interlining as shown in diagram 2.

Fold the remaining fabric to enclose
the interlining and machine stitch in
place on the right-hand side of the
interlining (diag 2).

Turn to the right side and fold the
flap in along the stitchline. There
should be a 2cm (¾") seam allowance
at the left-hand short end (diag 3).

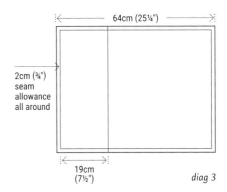

2cm (¾")
seam
allowance
all around

64cm (25¼")

19cm
(7½")

diag 3

Trim the seam allowance to 1.5cm
(⅝") all around, mitre the corners and
cut away the excess fabric.

Apply a thin layer of craft glue along
the edge of the seam allowance on
each straight edge. Fold in the seam
allowance and finger press in place.

6   Match the lining to the beaded fabric
and hold in place with clips. Ladder
stitch together beginning with the
upper and lower edges followed by
the unbeaded short end.

Glue the remaining 1cm magnets
between the beaded piece and lining
along the beaded band placing one
in the centre and one on each outer
edge. While the glue is still wet,
check that the poles and positions are
correctly matched. Allow to dry.

Ladder stitch the remaining edge.

7   Fold the folio and fasten with the
magnets. Gently steam along the
folded edges to shape.

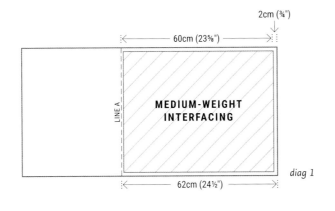

2cm (¾")

60cm (23⅝")

LINE A

**MEDIUM-WEIGHT
INTERFACING**

62cm (24½")

diag 1

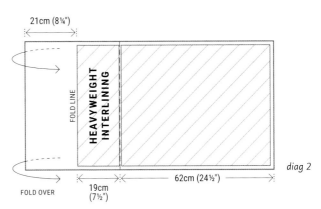

21cm (8¼")

FOLD LINE

**HEAVYWEIGHT
INTERLINING**

FOLD OVER

19cm
(7½")

62cm (24½")

diag 2

"Every project begins with a clean length of fabric on an embroidery frame, stitched in and stretched tight like a drum skin. I have been learning Japanese embroidery and bead embroidery from Margaret for a few years now, but that feeling of tense expectation is always the same. And this was the first time I would be designing a project in collaboration with Margaret, so I felt an added pressure for my ideas and craft to live up to expectation.

I came to her with the idea of covering a journal. Margaret knows I've always had a strong preference for geometric patterns and the strong, stylised Japanese designs. The ground fabric would need to be darker as there would not be a lot of background beading. I told Margaret I liked the idea of blue. She found an indigo slub silk that perfectly suited the project and first design drawings of the Japanese noshi.

It was important that the design choices reflected the traditional use of Japanese symbols and patterns, even though the materials were being used differently. Some ideas planned early on to fill the noshi were not in the final piece with a change made in bead choice or design after experimenting. This was challenging for me, as I have always liked to have everything planned and decided in advance. And yet, with plenty of advice and encouragement, I stitched.

The first step in Japanese projects is the element of the design that is 'on top'. Outlining the cord knot of the noshi in silver couching thread felt comfortable and familiar. Next, I began stitching over the couching with a new multi-coloured metal thread—something new to learn.

Margaret then suggested bugle beads for the outlines of some of the ribbons to help bring them to the front of the design. I had only stitched bugle beads as random before, and I found it difficult at first to keep a smooth line. But I was surprised how quickly I covered the lines once I got the knack.

The kikko was the first pattern I completed. Standing back from the fabric, it now made sense to me why the design drawings had so many blank areas. Design decisions like that could only be made along the way as we saw the pattern gradually reveal itself. The fuzzy ribbon in the background was an example of this: the space it filled was not clear until surrounding elements were in place.

Margaret showed me how to stitch the seigaiha pattern many times. I spent a lot of time stitching down beads and taking them out, until in frustration I moved on to other parts of the design. When I came back to it, I experimented with stitching the beads in another direction and mixing up the sizes of the beads to create 'flow' in the waves. I presented my solution to Margaret, keen to maintain the conventions of Japanese traditional stitching.

The final part of the design to be realised was the very front ribbon. Margaret and I discussed the different possibilities to fill this area, then she sent me a few different patterns of tatewaku (Steam Rising) for me to choose from. I went through many different combinations of beads, and I played around with the size of these designs—using a photocopier and cutting them out and placing them over the design—until I was satisfied.

The feeling of placing the final beads on a project is another moment which I still feel as keenly as when I first began. It's a time to reflect on all that I have learned about the practices of Japanese embroidery and on the new skills I have developed. And yet I know that my next project will be to stitch this noshi with silks. Already I can't wait to be faced with a taut new length of silk."

Frances Langenberg

A DIFFERENT INTERPRETATION

The alternative project is stitched by Carol James who opted to frame it. Carol embroidered some of the *noshi* strips with traditional silk embroidery as she envisioned incorporating the various Japanese embroidery skills that she had acquired into one design. In fact, she is looking to stitch a partner piece to this one. The design for this is still in its incubation stage.

Here is Carol's embroidery story.

"My bead embroidery journey began roughly nine years ago when I went to Margaret to learn Chinese embroidery. I was inspired by other student's work in Japanese Embroidery, and I then

decided this was going to be my next challenge. Whilst working on my first Japanese piece, Margaret showed the class a beautiful, beaded glasses case that I fell in love with. Yes, that is where my love for beading began. As with most of Margaret's beautiful pieces in embroidery, they are challenging but satisfying. I began multi-tasking working on a couple of projects at the same time. With the bead embroidery, working with double needles and koma is a unique skill to learn. I found beading very relaxing and rewarding and have since completed seven projects.

Inspiration struck and I wondered if beading, Chinese and Japanese embroidery could be combined. I discussed this with Margaret as I envisioned a framed

picture that incorporated beading and embroidery on my wall. Margaret again far exceeded my expectations with this elegant and meaningful noshi design which included beading, goldwork, and Japanese embroidery.

It was a tremendous pleasure to work with Margaret in choosing colours and stitches to bring the design to realisation. This project was such a joy to work on and I just love it.

Words cannot express how thankful I am to Margaret for this fantastic design and her encouragement. I feel like a queen who has been given the crown jewels. The project will have pride of place on the wall.

Awaiting now the sequel to join it."

TROPICANA

Floral patterns have featured in textiles in almost every culture in one form or another, seemingly eternal and never out of fashion. They are depicted in their natural state, in stylised and impressionist forms with each generation and culture adding their own unique historical stamp - think William Morris, embroidered silk peonies from China, Venetian floral lace, Indian chintz and silk brocades of 17th and 18th century Europe, tulips and pomegranates of 16th and 17th century Persia and so the list goes on into the modern era.

In this project, exotic tropical ginger plants, ferns and flowers, provide the inspiration. They evoke nostalgic and happy memories of my childhood in the tropics. The strong bright colours associated with the tropics are also used.

tropicana

POINTS OF INTEREST

The variety of flowers and foliage in
the design requires careful selection
of bead type, finishes and colours to
ensure that they are not only individually
showcased but work together within the
design to produce the requisite balance,
movement, linear and dimensional
perspectives as well as textural interest.

Size of the leaf patterns is noteworthy.
They are comparable in size to many of
the flowers. Not only are they sizeable
but also lush and abundant, as would
be the case in the tropics. Additionally,
the leaves are either presented in groups
or near proximity to one another. This
presents a challenge to ensure they do
not overwhelm the flowers or take over
the overall design. The strategy adopted
to overcome this was to create a degree
of individuality between the leaves.

In complex designs such as this, a
colour plan is encouraged. Colour in key
elements on paper, paying attention to
which elements to highlight and which to
recede. The colour plan provides an initial
visual check for overall colour balance,
movement, and perspective. It also
facilitates bead and technique selection.
See the Flower and Leaf Guide for the
colour plan used for this project. Refer to
this chart as well in conjunction with the
instructions during stitching.

Note the use of negative space in some
design elements. The planned negative
spaces are coloured with metallic gold
and blue to complement the embroidery.

Practical consideration is also given to
the final use. As the finished project will
be made into a purse, flowers situated
along the spine of the wallet are subject
to more wear. Techniques used for these
elements should be well thought out.

Red backgrounds are challenging to work
with but felt right given the theme of
the design. The primary colour scheme
of red, yellow and blue was selected to
create an underlying atmosphere of
vibrancy and energy.

The finished purse measures
11cm x 20cm wide (4 ⅜" x 8").

Techniques Used:

*Couching technique 1 – combination
needle-koma*

Diagonal single layer

Line of held thread – straight line

Line of held thread – circle

Line of held thread – curved line

*Line of staggered diagonals – metallic
thread*

Japanese running stitch

Raised effect – general padding

Scatter effect technique – singles

Separated single layer

Simple five-petal flower

*Single stitch with one and multiple
beads*

Vertical single layer

64

Fabric and supplies

30cm x 27cm wide (12" x 10½") piece of mottled red cotton

24cm x 20cm wide (9½" x 8") piece of 1mm adhesive felt

Red zipped purse frame

50wt off-white cotton sewing thread

50wt red cotton sewing thread

50wt sapphire blue cotton sewing thread

50wt leaf green cotton sewing thread

12wt red *Wonderfil* Egyptian cotton thread

Jacquard Lumiere metallic paint 561 gold

Pebeo setacolor fabric paint metallic blue

Size 3 acrylic paint brush

Size 5 acrylic paint brush

Needles

No. 3 milliner's
No. 7 sharp
No. 11 sharp
No. 12 sharp

Beads and thread

*Bead quantities listed refer to a
5cm x 12mm (2" x ⅜") tube*

CZECH 2mm FIRE-POLISHED BEADS
A = patina copper bronze (7 pieces)

CZECH 3mm FIRE-POLISHED BEADS
B = jonquil (6 pieces)
C = sapphire blue (3 pieces)

PRECIOSA SIZE 9 3-CUT BEADS
D = emerald lustre (40 pieces)

PRECIOSA SIZE 12 3-CUT BEADS
E = green iris (40 pieces)
F = green lustre (1)

TOHO SIZE 8 SEED BEADS
G = 284 inside colour aqua gold-lined (10 pieces)
H = 557 perma-finish galvanised starlight (½)

TOHO SIZE 11 SEED BEADS
I = 1 transparent crystal (20 pieces)
J = 3B transparent dk aquamarine (¼)
K = 13 transparent lt sapphire (⅓)
L = 22 silver-lined lt topaz (⅓)
M = 22C silver-lined topaz (⅓)
N = 108 transparent lustre peridot (¼)
O = 162 transparent rainbow lt topaz (⅓)
P = 165B transparent rainbow Siam ruby (20 pieces)
Q = 167 transparent rainbow peridot (10 pieces)
R = 284 inside colour aqua gold-lined (¼)
S = 341 inside colour crystal tomato-lined (⅓)
T = 557 perma-finish galvanised starlight (¼)
U = 779 inside colour rainbow crystal salmon-lined (⅓)
V = 901 Ceylon rice pudding (½)

TOHO SIZE 15 SEED BEADS
W = 2B transparent med topaz (⅛)
X = 3B transparent dk aquamarine (⅛)
Y = 13 transparent lt sapphire (1/4)
Z = 22 silver-lined lt topaz (½)
AA = 22C silver-lined topaz (¼)
AB = 45 opaque pepper red (¼)
AC = 108 transparent lustre peridot (⅛)
AD = 148 Ceylon peach cobbler (⅛)
AE = 162B transparent rainbow med topaz (⅛)
AF = 162C transparent rainbow topaz (⅛)

AG = 178 transparent rainbow sapphire (¼)
AH = 284 inside colour aqua gold-lined (⅛)
AI = 290 transparent lustre rose (¼)
AJ = 341 inside colour crystal tomato-lined (¼)
AK = 388 inside colour lt topaz orange-lined (⅛)
AL = 459 gold lustre dk topaz (⅓)
AM = 557 perma-finish galvanised starlight (⅛)
AN = 779 inside colour rainbow crystal salmon-lined (¼)
AO = 932 inside colour aqua Capri-lined (⅛)

TOHO SIZE 12 3-CUT BEADS
AP = 45 opaque pepper red (1½)
AQ = 103 transparent lustre lt topaz (¼)
AR = 162B transparent rainbow med topaz (¼)
AS = 290 transparent lustre rose (¼)
AT = 421 gold lustre transparent pink (⅓)
AU = 932 inside colour aqua Capri-lined (¼)

TOHO SIZE 15 3-CUT BEADS
AV = 421 gold lustre transparent pink (⅓)

TOHO 3mm BUGLE BEADS
AW = 22 silver-lined lt topaz (20 pieces)

SIZE 1 JAPANESE METAL THREAD
AX = gold

Flower with pointed petal – Variation 2 – Colour option 1   Leaves - Variation 2 – Light green leaves with white thread   Flower with pointed petal – Variation 2 – Colour option 2

Blue leaves with sapphire threads   Dark green leaves with light sapphire threads   Ferns 1   Ferns 2   Leaves variation 1 – Apply metallic blue paint

Apply gilding   Gold star shaped flower   Rounded petal flower with padding   Flower with pointed petals – Variation 1 – Colour option 1   Blue leaves

Rounded petal flower with no padding   Flower with pointed petals – Variation 1 – Colour option 2   Medium green leaves – Variation 2 with light sapphire threads

A – Complex Flower 1   **B** – Complex flower 2   **C** – Complex flower 3   **D** – Complex flower 4   **E** – Fancy large leaf   **F** – Flower spray

FLOWER AND LEAF GUIDE

DESIGN AND PATTERN PREPARATION

See the liftout pattern for the embroidery design.

Preparing the fabric

On the wrong side, mark the fabric warp with thread or a removable fabric marker.

Transferring the design

Transfer the design referring to page 122. Mount the fabric on the frame referring to pages 123–125. Mark in the outline with thread using *line of held thread technique* for straight sections and *Japanese running stitch* for curved sections.

ORDER OF WORK

Colouring and gilding the fabric

Using the guide, paint the elements with the acrylic brushes, diluting the gold paint before applying a light wash. The metallic blue should be applied to fully obscure the red fabric.

Flowers with pointed petals – variation 1

Large flower centre

Stitch a single **C** at the centre and surround with single **L**, placing the stitches at the cardinal points then adding a bead in each quarter.

Small flower centre

Stitch a single **AU** at the centre of the small flower and surround with **L** using *line of held thread – circle technique*.

Petals

Each flower comprises six petals. After stitching the first petal, work the two alternate petals, abutting the flower centre. Complete the remaining three petals, finishing each stitch where the design line ends.

Outline each petal on the lighter flower with **U**, tapering at each end with 1–2 x

AN using *line of held thread – curved line method*. Work a single stitch down the centre of the petal with 1 x **U** and the required number of **AN** to complete the line. Stitch the darker flowers in a similar manner using **S** and **AJ**, omitting **S** from the centre stitch of the small flower.

Bud

Stitch the calyx and stem on the bud with 2 x **AC** and the required number of **Z** using *line of held thread – curved line method*. Tie down each bead. Work four stitches fanning out from the calyx, beginning the first stitch at the centre aligned with the calyx then adding two outer stitches and the fourth stitch on one side between the centre and outer stitch. Use **S** with **AJ** at each end to taper or **AJ**.

Flowers with pointed petals – variation 2

Centre

Stitch a single **AU** at the centre of each darker pink flower and encircle with **AA** using *line of held thread – circle method*. Stitch a single **J** at the centre of the lighter pink flower and encircle with **Z** in the same manner.

Petals

Each flower has five or six petals.

Using *raised effect – general padding technique*, pad each petal with three horizontal stitches with **AN**, working a stitch with one bead at the tip then two stitches with two beads. Leave a bead

space between the padding and the edge of the petal. The padding should extend ⅔ down from the petal tip. Work each petal on the darker flowers with **Z**, **U** and **AN** using *vertical single layer technique*. Each petal has 4–5 stitches. Begin with a stitch down the centre of the petal then work a stitch on each side of the centre, ensuring a neat point with accurate stitch placement, using 3 x **Z** at the tip of the centre stitch and 1–2 x **Z** at the tip of the side stitches. Add one or two stitches on the outer edges of the petal, bringing the needle up and down just inside the edge of the previous stitches to achieve a neat tip and rounded shape for the petal. Use **AN** on each end to taper the stitches. **U** can be omitted from these stitches to achieve the correct shape. A smaller version of this flower is worked using only **AN** to stitch the petals.

Work the light pink flower petals in a similar manner using **AI** and **AS**.

Bud

Stitch the calyx with two straight stitches forming a V shape with **Q** and **F** at each end to taper. If the number of beads must be reduced to fit the length, omit the bead at the base of the calyx. Pad and stitch the bud in a similar manner to the padded petals, using **AN** for the padding. Work the centre stitch with 2 x **AN**, 3 x **U** and the required number of **Z** to complete the line.

Work the remaining stitches with **AN** and **U**.

Flowers with pointed petals – variation 1

Flowers with pointed petals – variation 2

Rounded petal flowers

Rounded-petal flowers

There are three flowers that are stitched in a similar manner. The flower that sits on the spine is not padded.

Centre

Stitch a single **Q** at the centre and surround with single **P**, placing the stitches oriented north and south then adding two, evenly spaced beads in each half.

Petals

Using **raised effect – general padding technique**, work two stitches across each petal with **AE** using enough beads so that a bead space remains between the ends of the stitch and the edge of the petal. Stitch each petal using vertical single layer technique beginning with the centre stitch with **O** and **AE**. Use **O** up to the ⅔ mark of the petal then add the required **AE** to complete the stitch. Work stitches in the same manner on each side until there are five stitches. Tuck the outermost stitches slightly beneath the adjacent stitches to create a rounded shape. Tie down to shape. Stitch the flower without padding in a similar manner using **AQ** and **W**.

Complex flower 1

Flower

Stitch a single **A** at the base of the flower and encircle with **AM** using **line of held thread – circle method**.

Stitch the two beads at the top of the flower as a single stitch with **T** and **B** and tie down between the beads. Outline the flower with **AT** *using couching technique 1 – combination needle-koma method.*

Work two rows of crossover stitches down the centre of the flower with **AV**. Work straight stitches with the same beads down the centre with each stitch crossing the intersections where the crossover stitches meet. Fill the remaining area on each side of the centre with diagonal stitches with **L** tapering to **Z** where necessary and beginning at the base and working to the tip. Add single lines at the base of the flower with **Z**, working the longer lines **using couching technique 1 – combination needle-koma method** and the short lines using **line of held thread – curved line method**.

Leaves

Work the leaves at the top of the flower using **separated single layer technique** with **Z** and **AG** for the blue leaves and **Z** and **F** for the green leaves, using **Z** for the veins.

Stamens

Work the filaments with **AX**, half-hitched onto the needle to create a double thread, using **line of staggered diagonals technique.**

Add single random stitches with **H**, **T** and **AM** to form the anthers.

Complex flower 2

Corolla

Stitch the lower section of the corolla, working fanned straight stitches, beginning with the centre stitch with 2 x **AT** and the required number of **AV** to complete and taper the stitch. Work stitches on alternate sides in the same manner. Stitch the top of the corolla with single stitches of varying lengths radiating around the shape. Use 1 x **AO** at the base of each stitch and the required number of **AU**. Fill the centre of the corolla using **scatter effect technique – singles** with **Z**.

Petals

Stitch from the foreground to the background. Outline each petal using **couching technique 1 – combination needle-koma method** for the longer lines and **line of held thread – curved line method** for the short lines with **M** tapering to **AA** at each end. Work the petal markings with straight stitches using **AA**, beginning with the long centre line and fitting shorter lines on each side using **line of held thread – straight and curved line method.**

Complex flower 3

Petals

Stitch the foreground leaf-shaped petal using **separated single layer technique** with **Z** for the centre vein and **AL**. Outline the side petals, beginning with the foreground section and working each section separately using **couching technique 1 – combination needle-koma method** for the longer lines and **line of held thread – curved line method** for the short lines. Stitch with **AT** and **AV** using **AT** only in the top line of each petal. Work the petal markings using **line of held thread – curved line method**, stitching the centre line first with 2 x **L** at the tip and the required number of **Z**. Add a

Complex flower 1

Complex flower 2

Complex flower 3

short line on each side of the centre with 1 x **L** at the tip and the required number of **Z** to complete the line. Tie down to shape. Work the overlapping scales using *line of held thread – curved line method* with **Z**. Stitch a single **AS** at the centre of each scallop shape

Centre

Stitch a single **AU** at the centre of the flower.

Complex flower 4

Petals

Stitch single lines fanning from the base of the stamens on the inner petal with **L** tapering to **Z** at the centre. Work the frilled petal edge with random short curved lines *using line of held thread – curved line method* with **AV**, either meeting or overlapping the ends. Stitch the outer petals in the same manner as the Pointed petal flowers – variation 2 using **Z** for the padding and **AF** and **AR**.

Stamens

Work the filaments with **AX**, half-hitched onto the needle to create a double thread, using *line of staggered diagonals technique*. Add single random stitches with **T** and **AM** to form the anthers.

Ferns 1

Beginning at the tip, pick up enough **AL** to work the lower edge of the frond and enough **Z** to work the remaining stem to the base. Stitch in place using *couching technique 1 – combination needle-koma method*. Work the lower edge of the remaining fronds with **AL** using *couching technique 1 – combination needle-koma method* for the longer lines and *line of held thread – curved line method* for the short lines. Complete each frond with **AL** using *diagonal single layer technique*, beginning at the tip. Use right diagonals for the left-hand fronds and left diagonals for the right-hand fronds.

Ferns 2

Work single stitches with **R** and **AH**, tapering with 1–2 x **AH** at the base of each stitch and one bead at some tips. Stitch the centre vein using *line of staggered diagonals technique* with **AX** half-hitched on the needle to create a double thread.

Fancy large leaf

Base and stem

Outline the base with two stitches, each using *line of held thread – straight line technique* with 1–2 x **AH**, 1 x **R**, 2 x **G**, 1 x **R** and 1 x **AH**. Stitch the stem with **R** using *couching technique 1 – combination needle-koma method*. Work an arc within the V shape with **Z** using *line of held thread – curved line method*. Stitch a single **B** at the centre of the shape. Work single stitches with **AW** and **Z** fanning out along the top of the arc, beginning with the centre stitch followed by the outermost stitches. Add two, evenly spaced stitches on each side.

Outline

Stitch the outline with **AL** using *line of held thread – curved line method* working from the tip down one side then the other.

Work the small fern centre lines with **AH** using *couching technique 1 – needle-koma method*. Complete each frond with single diagonal stitches with 2–3 x **AH**.

Stitch the *simple five-petal flowers* with **AT** for the centre and **T** for the petals. Work the fan at the tip of the leaf with a single **B** aligned with the stem, and five stitches fanning from **B**, beginning with the centre stitch, followed by two stitches on each side with **Z** using *line of held thread – straight line technique*. Stitch a single **AU** between the fern and the fan.

Leaves

Variation 1 with painted background

Beginning at the leaf tip, work each scallop section with **K**, tapering with **Y** and the sapphire blue sewing thread using *line of held thread – curved line method*. Stitch the centre vein, beginning at the tip, with 3 x **AK** and the required number of **Z** with off-white sewing thread using *couching technique 1 – combination needle-koma method*. Couch between each bead. Work the side veins with single diagonal stitches with **AK** using *line of held thread – straight and curved line method* and off-white sewing thread.

Complex flower 4   *Ferns 1*   *Ferns 2*   *Fancy large leaf*   *Leaves - Variation 1 with painted background*

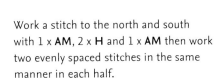

Variation 2

Each leaf is worked using *separated single layer technique*. Stitch each leaf vein with **Z**.

Work the light green leaves with **F** and off-white sewing thread, the medium green leaves with **F** and sapphire blue sewing thread and the dark green leaves with **N**, **I** and **AC** and sapphire blue sewing thread. **I** is used within one or two lines in the mid-section. Use only **AC** for the smaller dark green leaf.

Stitch the blue leaves with **K** and **Y** with the sapphire blue sewing thread.

Flower spray

Flowers

Stitch a single **L** at each flower centre. Work the flowers as *simple five-petal flowers* with **U** or eight-petal flowers with **U** and **AN**. Stitch the buds with a single **U** or group of 3 x **U**.

Leaves

Work each leaf with a single stitch with 1 x **E** at each end and the required number of **D**, varying from 1–3.

Stems

Stitch the stems with **AX** half-hitched onto the needle to create a double thread using *line of staggered diagonals technique*.

Background flowers

Gold star-shape flowers

Stitch a single **A** at the centre of each flower.

Work a stitch to the north and south with 1 x **AM**, 2 x **H** and 1 x **AM** then work two evenly spaced stitches in the same manner in each half.

Eight-petal flower

Stitch a single **AT** at the centre and work the petals with **AD** and **V** on the outer edge.

Five-petal flower

Work a *simple five-petal flower* with **AT** for the centre and **V** for the petals.

Background

The background is filled with *scatter effect technique – singles* in two stages.

Begin filling the background from the centre working outwards with **AP** and **AB** in tight, tapered spaces, stopping at the edge of the beaded motifs. Re-measure the outline to ensure that it remains 22.5cm x 19.5cm wide (8 7/8" x 7 11/16") and adjust if necessary.

Complete filling the background to the marked outline.

Leaves - Variation 2

Flower spray

Gold star shaped flower

Eight-petal flower

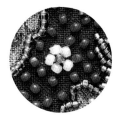

Five-petal flower

CONSTRUCTION

Refer to the construction diagrams for
Enchanted.

All seam allowances are 1cm (³⁄₈").

1. Complete the finishing process
    referring to page 132.

2. Using the black pen, transfer the felt
    template shaping to tracing paper
    and cut out. Pin the template to the
    felt and cut out.

3. Place the beaded fabric in the frame,
    wrong side uppermost, onto a towel
    over a hard surface. Peel away the
    backing paper and position the felt,
    adhesive side down, over the wrong
    side of the embroidery and press
    gently. Check to ensure that the felt
    is positioned correctly. The stitching
    marking the outline should be
    visible outside the felt.

    Apply pressure to the felt in a
    sweeping motion from the centre
    outwards to ensure it is securely
    attached. Remove the fabric from
    the frame. Leaving a 1cm (³⁄₈") seam
    allowance, cut out.

    Beginning and ending 2cm (³⁄₄")
    from one corner, work a line of small
    running stitches with the off-white
    sewing thread, 5mm (³⁄₁₆") from the
    raw edge.

    Pull up the thread until the fabric
    gathers neatly behind the corner
    and secure. Repeat on the remaining
    corners. Fold under the seam
    allowance along each straight edge
    and tack in place using the same
    thread. The beads at the edge of the
    design should sit slightly over the
    folded edge of the fabric.

4. Mark the centre on the upper and
    lower short edges of the beaded

fabric and on both sides of the zip
on the purse frame.

Cut a 50cm (20") length of 12wt red
Wonderfil thread.

Match the marked points of the
beaded fabric and zip. Secure the
thread at the halfway point into the
seam allowance of the beaded fabric
close to the marked centre with two
back stitches.

Beginning at the marked centre
point, ladder stitch the beaded
fabric to the zip tape, working 3mm
(¹⁄₈") above the stitched line on the
tape. Stitch to 1.5cm (⁵⁄₈") past the
rounded corner and unthread the
needle, leaving the excess thread
hanging.

Return to the starting point and
thread the remaining half into the
needle. Attach the second half of the
fabric to the zip in the same manner,
again leaving the remaining thread
hanging.

Turn the purse to the second side
and attach the second end of the
fabric to the zip in the same manner.

Re-thread one of the hanging threads
and continue attaching the fabric to
the zip with ladder stitch, stitching
up to the zip teeth then back along
the seam for 1cm (³⁄₈") to reinforce
the stitching. Secure the thread and
trim away any excess. Complete the
remaining three sections using the
remaining hanging threads in the
same manner.

5. Gently massage the finished purse
    with your fingers to mould the fit.
    Steam the purse gently and give it a
    final moulding with your fingers.

    Allow to dry.

A DIFFERENT
INTERPRETATION

Robyn Fererro stitched the alternate project,
and it cannot be more different to the
sample. She has a wonderful colour sense
and had no idea about the colour scheme
I planned with the sample and I wanted to
give her free rein. All I asked for was her
choice of colour for the ground fabric.

The result is a great example of how
colours can totally change the atmosphere of
a design. While the sample project portrays
vibrancy, sunshine and bright colours of the
tropics, Robyn's colour scheme produces
a feeling of elegance and summer colours
of temperate zones. In keeping with the

ambience of her project, the fancy large leaf no longer looked right. She adjusted this to suit the overall design. Look a little closer and you will also see other adjustments. Robyn has put her creativity to great effect.

Here is what Robyn has to say about her project.

"When I was offered the opportunity to contribute to this book, I was honoured but scared. My 'creativity' in my view was low but I hoped to not disappoint Margaret.

I wanted the design of my project to reflect my love of all things floral and summer.

I also wanted it to be a practical and useful item that would give pleasure to the owner for years to come.

The design was initiated by a drawing by Margaret and we discussed colour combinations and techniques to bring the piece to life. As this book is designed to encourage creativity it was important to instil my own ideas relating to the design, colour and placement of the flowers. This proved to be more of a challenge than I had expected!

The greatest challenge I faced was to balance the colours and texture for a piece that would be handled and used everyday for years. This meant that limited height

dimensions were required to ensure the purse would last the distance.

Floral designs typically require raised techniques such as padding to enhance the flow of the design. I believed that this meant colours and placement of the elements had to be carefully co-ordinated to achieve the effect I had imagined. This involved MUCH stitching and unpicking. At one stage I was so fed up I asked if I could ditch this project and do another, Margaret said no! Finally, I completed the project and I would like to thank Margaret for encouraging me to explore the creative process."

Robyn Ferrero

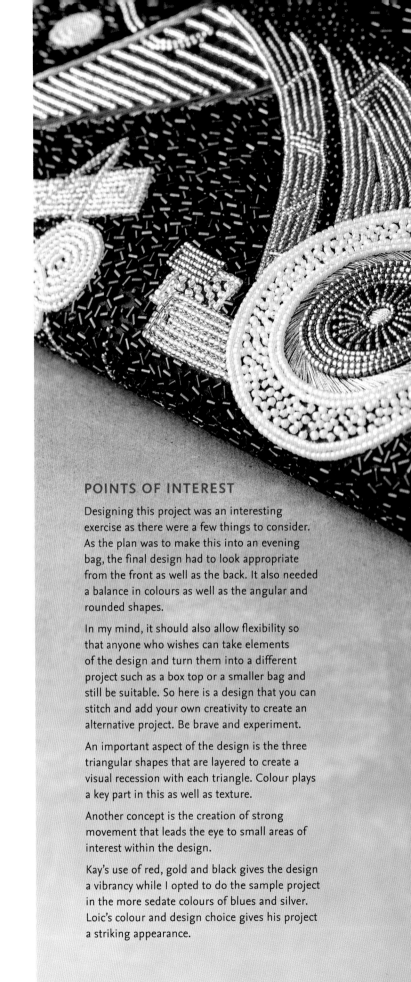

AFTER KANDINSKY

The question has always been asked if Japanese embroidery or Japanese-style bead embroidery can be used for geometric designs. The answer is an emphatic 'yes' as many traditional *wagara* patterns are geometrically created.

What about more modern geometric patterns? As a matter of fact, Japanese textile designs were influenced by the Western Art Deco movement of the 1920s to early 1930s. The geometric designs of the period were incorporated onto obi and kimono and even transferred to other accessories such as collars, combs and hairpins.

When I asked Loic Jeanneau if he would like to stitch a project for the book, he mentioned the art of Wassily Kandinsky which piqued my interest and resulted in the design offered here. This design is also stitched in an alternative colour-way by Kay Jenkins and Loic worked on a design that he conceived. These projects demonstrate geometric designs are certainly compatible with Japanese-style bead embroidery with careful planning.

I have titled the project *After Kandinsky* in recognition of the borrowed design concept from the pioneer of abstraction in Western art.

POINTS OF INTEREST

Designing this project was an interesting exercise as there were a few things to consider. As the plan was to make this into an evening bag, the final design had to look appropriate from the front as well as the back. It also needed a balance in colours as well as the angular and rounded shapes.

In my mind, it should also allow flexibility so that anyone who wishes can take elements of the design and turn them into a different project such as a box top or a smaller bag and still be suitable. So here is a design that you can stitch and add your own creativity to create an alternative project. Be brave and experiment.

An important aspect of the design is the three triangular shapes that are layered to create a visual recession with each triangle. Colour plays a key part in this as well as texture.

Another concept is the creation of strong movement that leads the eye to small areas of interest within the design.

Kay's use of red, gold and black gives the design a vibrancy while I opted to do the sample project in the more sedate colours of blues and silver. Loic's colour and design choice gives his project a striking appearance.

after kandinsky

The finished purse measures
14.5cm x 24cm wide (5⅜" x 9½").

Techniques Used:

*Couching technique 1 – combination
needle-koma*

Couching technique 3 – to and fro

Couching technique 4 – round and round

Diagonal single layer – metallic thread

Horizontal single layer – metallic thread

Japanese running stitch

Line of held thread – circle

Line of held thread – curved line

Line of held thread – straight line

Long and short stitch

Scatter effect technique – singles

*Single stitches with one and
multiple beads*

Vertical single layer – metallic thread

Fabric and supplies

50cm x 70cm wide (20" x 27½") navy
silk taffeta

58cm x 25cm wide (23" x 10") piece of
fusible heavyweight interlining

26cm x 20cm wide (10⅛" x 8") piece of
fusible medium-weight interfacing

25cm x 45cm wide (10" x 18")
piece of 1mm adhesive felt

50wt off-white cotton sewing thread

50wt black cotton sewing thread

50wt sapphire blue sewing thread

12wt black polyester sewing thread

2mm x 1.5cm (⅝") neodymium
magnets (3)

2mm x 1cm (⅜") neodymium
magnets (3)

Craft glue

E6000 industrial-strength adhesive

Needles

No. 26 chenille
No. 3 milliner's
No. 10 sharp
No. 12 sharp

Beads and thread

*Bead quantities listed refer to a 5cm x
12mm (2" x ½") tube*

CZECH 3mm FIRE-POLISHED BEADS
A = lt sapphire (22 pieces)

PRECIOSA SIZE 9 3-CUT BEADS
B = lt sapphire (1⅓)

PRECIOSA SIZE 12 3-CUT BEADS
C = lt sapphire (⅓)

TOHO SIZE 11 SEED BEADS
D = 21 silver-lined crystal (½)

E = 161 transparent rainbow crystal (½)
F = 168 transparent rainbow
lt sapphire (¾)
G = 178 transparent rainbow
sapphire (¾)
H = 192 inside colour crystal
yellow-lined (½)
I = 942 transparent sapphire (¾)
J = 565 perma-finish galvanised blue
slate (⅓)

TOHO SIZE 15 SEED BEADS
K = 9 transparent black diamond (⅓)
L = 21 silver-lined crystal (1¼)
M = 161 transparent rainbow crystal
(10 pieces)
N = 168 transparent rainbow lt
sapphire (¼)
O = 178 transparent rainbow
sapphire (½)
P = 565 perma-finish galvanised blue
slate (⅔)

TOHO SIZE 12 3-CUT BEADS
Q = 48 opaque navy blue (1)
R = 82 metallic nebula (½)
S = 101 transparent lustre crystal (½)
T = 142 Ceylon banana cream (1)

TOHO SIZE 15 3-CUT BEADS
U = 101 transparent lustre crystal (⅛)

TOHO 3mm BUGLE BEADS
V = 82 metallic nebula (5)

SIZE 1 JAPANESE METAL THREAD
W = silver multi-colour

DESIGN AND PATTERN PREPARATION

See the liftout pattern for the embroidery design.

Preparing the fabric

Cut a 50cm x 28cm wide (20" x 11") piece from the navy silk. On the wrong side, mark the warp edge with thread or a removable fabric marker. Cut a 50cm x 27cm wide (20" x 10⅝") piece for the bag lining and put aside.

The remaining 50cm x 15cm wide (20" x 6") is used for the gussets and gusset lining.

Transferring the design

Transfer the design referring to page 122.

Mount each fabric on a separate frame referring to pages 123–125.

Prepare the gussets in the same manner.

Mark the outline with thread using **line of held thread technique** for the straight sections and **Japanese running stitch** for the curved sections.

ORDER OF WORK

Metal thread

The thread is half-hitched to the needle, forming a double thread (diag 1).

Referring to the pattern guide for placement and stitch direction, fill the areas marked with blue with **W** using **diagonal single layer technique** in both right and left diagonal, **vertical single layer technique** and **horizontal single layer with self-padding technique**.

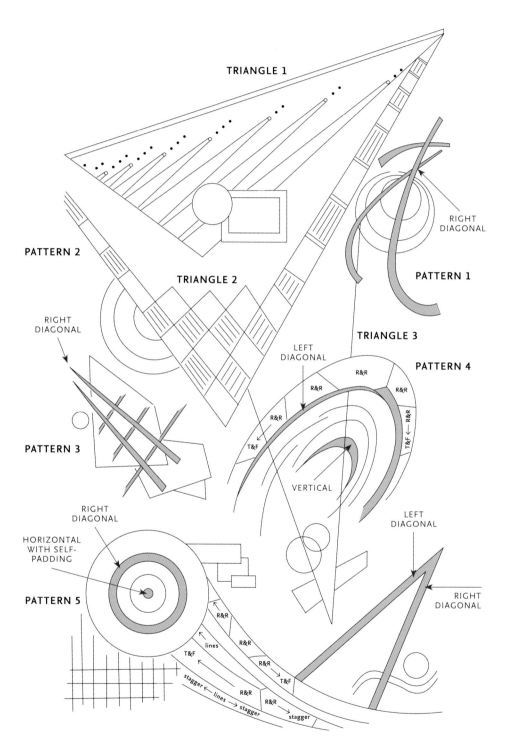

R&R – couching technique 4 - round and round
T&F – couching technique 3 - to and fro

PATTERN GUIDE

after kandinsky

Diagonal edge

Stitch the angled edge of the design with three rows of **V** using *line of held thread – straight line technique*.

Triangle 2

Work the outlines with *line of held thread – straight line technique* using **L**. Stitch the internal grid lines in the same manner, alternating the direction of the lines and beginning with the longest line.

Work alternate squares with parallel lines in a similar manner using **B** and **C**. Fill the remaining squares with closely worked *scatter effect technique – singles* using the same beads.

Triangle 1

Stitch the circle with rows of **H** beginning with a single bead at the centre and encircling with a row using *line of held thread – circle method*. Complete the remaining rows with *couching technique 1 – combination needle-koma method*.

Outline the rectangle with **S** using *couching technique 1 – combination needle-koma method* for the longer lines and *line of held thread – straight line technique* for the shorter lines. Add two inner lines in the same manner. Work the remaining triangle outline with **V** using *line of held thread – straight line technique*. Outline the long, narrow, internal triangles with **L** using *line of held thread – straight line technique*. Add single spaced beads at the end of each triangle with **D** and **L**. Work parallel lines across each triangle spaced 3mm (⅛") apart with **L** stitched with **W** using *line of held thread – straight line technique*. This replicates the *fuzzy effect technique* in traditional Japanese silk embroidery where the fabric shows between parallel lines of stitches.

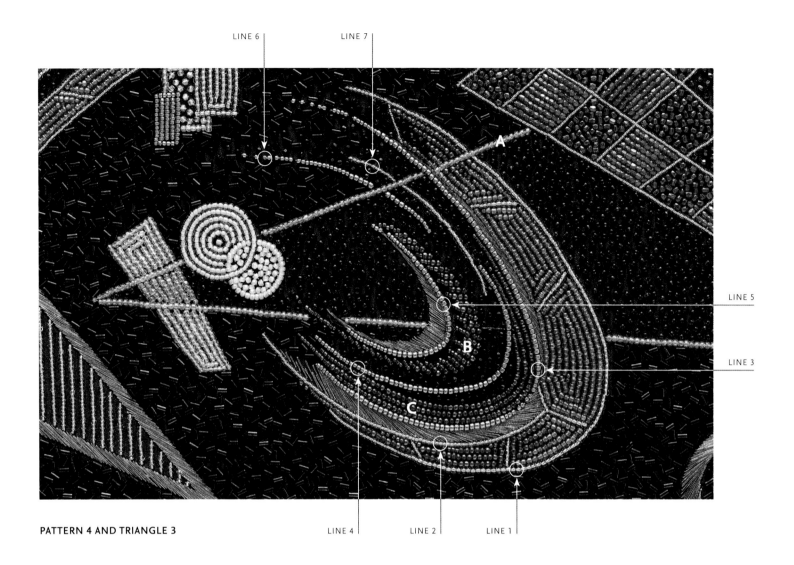

LINE 6 LINE 7

A

LINE 5

B

LINE 3

C

PATTERN 4 AND TRIANGLE 3

LINE 4 LINE 2 LINE 1

Pattern 1

Outline each side of the large circle with **T** using *couching technique 1 – combination needle-koma method*. Fill between the outlines with *scatter effect technique – singles* using the same beads. Outline the small circle with **P** using *couching technique 1 – combination needle-koma method* for the longer lines and *line of held thread – curved line method* for the short lines. Fill with *scatter effect technique – singles* using **K** and the blue sapphire thread. Fill the area between the circles in a similar manner using **Q**.

Pattern 2

Outline the innermost semi-circle with **T** using *couching technique 1 – combination*

needle-koma method. Fill the semi-circle with radiating lines using **G** and **O**, beginning with the line down the centre then alternating lines to each side and using the **O** beads at the inner edge to taper the lines. Work two lines around the outermost semi-circle with **P** on the outer line and **J** on the inner line using *couching technique 1 – combination needle-koma method*.

Work two lines around the middle semi-circle with **J** on the outer line and **S** on the inner line using *couching technique 1 – combination needle-koma method*. Fill the area between the inner and middle lines with *scatter effect technique – singles* using **T**. Stitch single, spaced **A** between the middle and outer lines.

Pattern 3

Outline the large, foreground shape using **D** for the top section tapering to **L** for the lower section using *line of held thread – straight line technique*.

Fill the shape with *scatter effect technique – singles* using **K** and the blue sapphire thread, increasing the density of the beads at the centre. Outline the medium shape with **S** using *line of held thread technique – straight line technique*. Fill the shape with *scatter effect technique – singles* using **S** and **U** towards the lower part of the shape. Outline and fill the small triangular shape with lines of beads using *line of held thread – straight line technique* and **P**. Stitch a single **H** at the centre of the small circle and surround with two rows of **H** using *line of held thread – circle method*.

Pattern 4 and triangle 3

Work the end of the short side of the triangle marked A with **E** stitched with **W** using *line of held thread – straight line technique*.

Stitch line 1 with **D** tapering into **L** at each end using couching *technique 1 – combination needle-koma method*. Stitch line 2 with **L** using the same technique and the internal dividing lines between lines 1 and 2 with **L** using *line of held thread – straight line technique*.

Fill the sections with **F**, **N**, **G** and **O** using *couching technique 1 – combination needle-koma method* stitching the sections at the ends with *couching technique 4 – round and round* or *couching technique 3 – to and fro*. Use **G** and **O** for shading towards the outer sections and **N** and **O** for tapering, staggering the ends on the outer edges.

Work line 3 in two sections beginning at the lower end of the line with **P**, changing to **J** using *couching technique 1 – combination needle-koma method*. At the curve taper with 3 x **P** then break the line and work two stitches with 2 x **P** one bead space apart. Restart the line with 5 x **P**, changing to **J**, tapering towards the end with **P**. Finish with spaced stitches reducing the number of beads from four to two to single beads.

Stitch line 4 with **J**, tapering at the ends with **P** using couching *technique 1 – combination needle-koma method*.

In the area between lines 3 and 4 (marked C), work three lines with **G** tapering to **O** using *couching technique 1 – combination needle-koma method*. Begin the first line next to line 3.

Work line 5 in a similar manner to line 3.

Stitch the area between line 4 and 5

(marked B), with **G** and **O**, using *long and short stitch technique* with **G** on the outer edge and tapering to **O** at the ends.

Work the overlapping circles, outlining the large circle first with **H** and the small circle with **T** using *couching technique 1 – combination needle-koma method*. Fill the large circle with rows of **H** in the same manner and the small circle with *scatter effect technique – singles* using **T**.

Stitch the remaining lines of triangle 3 with **E** stitched with **W** using *line of held thread – straight line technique*. Taper with a few **M** at the tip of the triangle.

Work line 6 with **J**, tapering at the ends to **P** using *couching technique 1 – combination needle-koma method*. Finish with spaced stitches reducing the number of beads from four to two to single beads.

Stitch line 7 with **D** tapering to **L** at each end using *couching technique 1 – combination needle-koma method*.

Fill the section of pattern 4 that falls outside the triangle with **R** using *scatter effect technique – singles*. Note that in the outer sections **R** changes to **V**.

Outline the shape at the tip of the triangle with **S** tapering to **U** at the narrow end of the shape and using *line of held thread – straight line technique*. Fill the shape with straight lines using the same beads and the sapphire blue thread for the area within the triangle, using **U** for the inner lines to fit the narrow end.

Pattern 5

Work an outline around the centre of the circle with **P** using *couching technique 1 – combination needle-koma method* combined with *line of held thread – circle technique*. Outline the next circle with **P** using *couching technique 1 – combination needle-koma method* then work three more circles with **J**. Fill the area around the centre with radiating lines with **G**

and **O**, positioning **G** on the outer edge of each line. Begin by working a line at each cardinal point then fill in with evenly divided stitches.

Outline each side of the outermost section of the circle with two rows of **T** using *couching technique 1 – combination needle-koma method*. Fill the space between the outlines with **T** using *scatter effect technique – singles*.

Using **L**, outline the curved sections emanating from the circle with *couching technique 1 – combination needle-koma method* and the lines dividing each section with *line of held thread – straight line technique*. Fill the sections with **F**, **N**, **G** and **O** using *couching technique 1 – combination needle-koma method* stitching the sections at the ends with *couching technique 4 – round and round* or *couching technique 3 – to and fro*. Use **G** and **O** for shading towards the outer sections and **N** and **O** for tapering, staggering the ends on the outer edges. Fill the remaining section with **R** using *scatter effect technique – singles*, transitioning into **V**.

Using **D**, outline the large rectangular shape with two rows and fill with three rows with *couching technique 1 – combination needle-koma method* for the long lines and *line of held thread – straight line technique* for the short lines. Outline the small rectangle with **P** and fill with three rows using *line of held thread – straight line technique*. Outline the medium rectangle with **S** using *line of held thread – straight line technique* and fill with *scatter effect technique – singles*.

Stitch the grid with **E** and **J** using **W** and gradating the colours between the two using *line of held thread – straight line technique*.

Pattern 6

Work the curved line with two rows of **J**, tapering to **P** at each end using *couching*

technique 1 – combination needle-koma method. Stitch the parallel lines across the triangular shape with **L** using *line of held thread – straight line technique* and increasing the spacing between the lines towards the base of the shape. Work the small circle with **H**, beginning with a single bead at the centre then working three circles of beads using *line of held thread – circle method*.

Background

Fill the background using the following beads and *scatter effect technique – singles*:

Triangle 1 – **V**
Triangle 2 – **Q**
Triangle 3 – **I**

Once complete, check the piece for sizing and adjust if necessary. Stitch spaced **V** along the outline. Complete the remaining background with **V** using *scatter effect technique – singles*.

Gussets

Stitch spaced **V** around the outline, omitting the bead at the centre of the upper straight edge. Stitch a second line of **V** across the upper straight edge, again omitting the bead at the centre. Stitch single **V** down the dotted lines.

CONSTRUCTION

All seam allowances are 1cm (⅝") unless specified.

––––––––––––––––––––––––––––––––

NOTE: Take care when cutting out the adhesive felt and fusible interlining to ensure that the flap shaping is oriented correctly.

––––––––––––––––––––––––––––––––

1   Complete the finishing process referring to page 132.

2   With the beading still on the frame, measure the beaded piece and check that the size remains true. Using the pattern template, cut out the adhesive felt 2mm (¹⁄₁₆") smaller than the template. Peel away the backing and position the felt, adhesive side down over the wrong side of the embroidery and press gently. Check to ensure that the felt is positioned correctly. The stitching marking the outline should be visible outside the felt. Apply pressure to the felt in a sweeping motion from the centre outwards to ensure it is securely attached. Remove the fabric from the frame and cut out leaving a 1.5cm (⅝") seam allowance. Clip the rounded edges. With the wrong side uppermost, apply a thin layer of craft glue to the edge of the seam allowance only. Fold in the seam allowance and glue in position. The outer line of beads will be visible. Using the lining template, mark in the gusset fold positions on the wrong side along the edge with thread or a removeable fabric marker.

3   Measure and mark the positions for the 1cm (⅜") magnets, 1.5cm (⅝") in from the angled edge of the flap at the midpoint and each end.

Using the industrial-strength adhesive, glue the larger magnets to the felt at the marked points.

Fold the beaded fabric into the finished bag position. Mark the positions on the main body of the bag, aligned with the magnets on the flap. Glue the 1.5cm (⅝") magnets in position on the felt side. Close the flap to ensure the positions are correct while the glue is wet and adjust if necessary. Hold the edges together with clips and allow to dry.

4   Cut out the fusible heavy interlining using the bag lining template. Fuse to the wrong side of the lining fabric. Leaving a 1cm (⅜") seam allowance, cut out the lining fabric. With the wrong side uppermost, apply a thin layer of craft glue to the edge of the seam allowance. Fold in the seam allowance and glue in position. Clip away excess fabric at the corners to remove bulk. Using the lining template, mark in the gusset/fold positions on the wrong side along the edge with thread or a removeable fabric marker.

5   Cut out four pieces of fusible medium interfacing using the gusset lining template.

Fuse one piece of interfacing to the wrong side of each beaded gusset. Cut out each gusset leaving a 1cm (⅜") seam allowance. Stitch the dart at the base of each gusset. Clip the rounded edges. With the wrong side uppermost, apply a thin layer of craft glue to the edge of the seam allowance. Fold in the seam allowance and glue in position.

6   Fuse the remaining two pieces of medium interfacing to the lining fabric and cut out leaving a 1cm (⅜") seam allowance. Prepare in the same manner as the beaded gussets.

7   With wrong sides together and matching edges, slipstitch each gusset and lining together around the outer edge.

8   With wrong sides together and matching edges and gusset/foldlines, slip stitch the bag and lining together along the short edge and long straight edges for 28cm (11") from the right-angle corner on each side.

9   Position one gusset on one side of the bag, aligning the dart with the gusset 1 position. Check to ensure that the top of the gusset will align with the square end of the bag on one side and the gusset 2 position on the other side when stitched in place.

Beginning at the base of the gusset and using the polyester sewing thread, ladder stitch one side of the gusset to the bag. Use clips to hold the gusset in place and prevent it from slipping while stitching. Return to the base and ladder stitch the second side in place.

10 Repeat with the second gusset.

11 Hold the lining and bag together at the centre of the open edge with a clip.

12 Holding the bag flap and lining together with clips in a curved position as if closing the bag, ladder stitch the lining and bag together along the remaining length of the long straight edges. Use several clips to ensure that the precise positions of the lining and bag are maintained.

13 Slip stitch the lining and bag together along the diagonal flap edge.

14 Place acid-free tissue paper inside the bag to hold the shape. Steam, paying attention to the gussets and flap fold-over. Finger press as required to shape.

15 Remove the paper and replace with dry tissue paper.

17 Leave the bag to dry overnight before use.

A DIFFERENT INTERPRETATION

The alternative projects created by Kay Jenkins and Loic Jeanneau are presented here and their comments on their creative journey speak for themselves.

Here is Kay's experience:

"Margaret Lee was my tutor at an embroidery convention more than a decade ago. At that stage I was largely self-taught in basic embroidery, had taken only a couple of embroidery classes and was, in reality, a beginner. I knew nothing of Japanese embroidery or Japanese bead embroidery, but the design of an eyeglass case appealed to me as it used both techniques. Little did I know at the time that this was the start of an

adventure with beads with Margaret that has brought me to today.

I have long had an affinity for beaded evening purses, preferably in black, but had never beaded an evening purse. I had altered designs in the past to suit my eye, but this was the first time I have been involved in the creation of the design in collaboration with Margaret who had suggested a very modern design based on the works of the artist Kandinsky. This was a bold step for me, and I was out of my comfort zone. The type of purse was the first decision to be made. For me, it had to be an evening purse and of a useful dimension.

I was attracted to the striking geometric design as laid out in the base drawings as it had the potential for a 'wow factor'. Discussions were held on the

layout of the multiple shapes of the drawing including how the shapes would appear on the purse flap, the area usually hidden beneath the flap and also the back. Coloured pencils were used to give an indicative view of the colour layout interspersed with notes about bead sizing, bead direction and techniques. The first step was to transfer the drawing to the black silk followed by painting some small areas of the design with gold fabric paint. The intention of the paint was to provide an element of change in colour to small areas of the black silk. This was new to me. At times, it was difficult for me to see how this design would rise from the luxurious but flat black silk but Margaret assured me, this was all part of the process of bringing the design to life.

Bead selection was a critical part of the overall process to try and give some interest and eye appeal to the multiple shapes on the line drawing. Margaret and I had fun choosing the beads – not everything originally chosen was used because the type of bead or the bead colour just looked out of place when stitched onto the fabric. The discussion moved to thread colour choice as subtle colour changes to the overall bead colour could be achieved by using a different colour thread. Having completed the planning work over a couple of months, the day finally came when I thought that the stitching with beads onto the black silk was to commence. Margaret then suggested firstly introducing some small areas of red metal thread for added interest, so I had to be patient for a while longer before that first bead was stitched onto the fabric. At Margaret's suggestion a couple of areas of 'fuzzy' were introduced as well. Fuzzy is a Japanese embroidery technique that was adapted to be used with beads for this purse.

For a while, I found it difficult to see how this design was going to translate into the anticipated eye-catching purse. Gradually, the coloured foreground work was completed and the design started to have a life. The background fabric started to look a little dull in comparison. As the background work using black beads was completed, I could see the piece really develop into something vibrant. The final step in the process (before construction) was the steaming of the finished piece whilst still under tension on the embroidery frame. Taking the piece off the embroidery frame and gently moulding it into the shape of the clutch purse, certainly reinforced my view that the beads did in fact zing and that the overall purse had a striking eye appeal.

My eye is drawn to the prominent front flap of the purse with its dramatic triangular shape edged in lines of black bugle beads. Under the flap there is a hidden area of one of the fuzzy triangles being quite prominent and finally the back of the purse has more triangles and an area of prominent curves. Light reflects differently across different areas of the purse, which adds to its appeal.

My sincere thanks to Margaret for firstly believing I could undertake this project and then giving me the opportunity to challenge myself with it. Margaret's advice and guidance to me were invaluable and greatly appreciated."

And from Loic…

"When Margaret asked me to collaborate with her I immediately said yes and soon after I was thrilled and scared at the same time. Scared because I've never done a project on my own. The choice of the final look of the embroidery came quickly in my head and that it must be an evening bag. Then I needed to find inspiration to realise that project. I've always been in admiration of the work of Wassily Kandinsky, especially his Composition number 8. I discussed with Margaret if I could work on something with geometric shapes/figures and she approved.

The inspiration was there and I needed to decide the main colour of the embroidery. I love the colour orange and Margaret said to me that she had an orange silk taffeta at home. She showed me a photo of it and it was settled. I had the source of inspiration and the main colour of the embroidery.

My journey started by drawing the design. Lots of questions came in my mind: what size should the bag be and what shape? How many geometric figures should I draw? …one big triangle, 2 big circles, 3 small circles, some lines running along, all are well placed on the bag shape. It was then time to take pencils and ink and colour all the shapes. The main colour was orange and I wanted to add some contrasting colours to it so the green and purple were mandatory and I added some pink, black and gold. At the end of that part I showed it to Margaret, she approved and I stepped into the next phase.

I transferred the design onto that gorgeous orange silk taffeta fabric. I had the main geometric figures on the fabric and I needed to decide how to stitch them. It was a tough moment for me and Margaret brought some ideas on how to stitch some parts of the design like the big circles and the chevron on the edges. Some other parts were quite clear in my head like the two small circles and the triangle shape. It was time to start stitching. So, I started to stitch the evening bag with a gorgeous purple Japanese metallic thread on the front circle. Then it was time to select and play with all the different beads I would use on the bag. Some adjustments had been made to the foreground geometric figures. For the background, I used only two techniques: the scatter effect and I really wanted to add a Japanese circle pattern called same komon. For these background parts it was important to select various kinds of beads to make them all different and give some dimension to the embroidery. Once all the design was stitched it was time to steam the embroidery before sewing all parts of the evening bag together.

From the beginning to the end of the project it was tough but not impossible. Tough because I've never done any project like this before. That experience gave me enough skills to do more projects like this in the future. I also must thank Margaret for her mentoring during all the process and the great opportunity she gave me to challenge myself."

POSH

Barbara Roberts is a fibre
specialist with expertise
in spinning, weaving, and
knitting besides a few other
things. We have had many
wonderful discussions on
textiles. I asked Barbara
to turn her creativity to
beading and presented her
with some proposed line
drawings to think about.
Here is the result.

The finished bag measures 42cm x 27cm wide (16½" x 10½").

Techniques Used:

Couching technique 1 – combination needle-koma

Diagonal single layer

Line of held thread – straight line

Line of held thread – curved line

Raised effect – general padding

Raised effect – stitch length adjustment

Scatter effect technique – singles

Single stitches with one and multiple beads

Vertical single layer

Fabric and supplies

75cm x 120cm wide (29½" x 47¼") piece of teal silk taffeta

56cm x 34cm wide (22" x 13½") piece of black lightweight woven interfacing

5cm x 4cm wide (2" x 1½") piece of lightweight fusible interfacing

32cm x 30cm wide (12½" x 12") piece of medium-weight fusible wadding

31cm (12¼") square of black adhesive vinyl

51cm x 41.5cm wide (20" x 16½") piece of black adhesive felt

50wt off-white cotton sewing thread

50wt dark teal cotton sewing thread

50wt dark green cotton sewing thread

Presencia Finca no. 8 perlé cotton col. 3670 (2)

Fibre-fill

Hexagonal box

Craft glue

Firm-bristle paint brush

Needles

No. 3 milliner's

No. 10 sharp

No. 12 sharp

Beads and thread

Bead quantities listed refer to a 5cm x 12mm (2" x ½") tube

CZECH 2mm FIRE-POLISHED BEADS
A = bronze (3 pieces)

CZECH 3mm FIRE-POLISHED BEADS
B = smoky topaz lustre (18 pieces)
C = turquoise AB (85 pieces)

CZECH 4mm FIRE-POLISHED BEADS
D = turquoise AB (85 pieces)

PRECIOSA SIZE 12 3-CUT BEADS
E = green iris (⅓)

TOHO SIZE 8 SEED BEADS
F = 22 silver-lined lt topaz (⅔)

TOHO SIZE 11 SEED BEADS
G = 6 transparent lt amethyst (⅓)
H = 161 transparent rainbow crystal (1)
I = 166B transparent rainbow med amethyst (⅓)
J = 166C transparent rainbow amethyst (⅓)
K = 551 perma-finish galvanised rose gold (⅓)

TOHO SIZE 15 SEED BEADS
L = 6 transparent lt amethyst (⅓)
M = 7 transparent peridot (½)
N = 82 metallic nebula (⅓)

O = 84 metallic iris green-brown (⅓)
P = 148 Ceylon peach cobbler (⅛)
Q = 161 transparent rainbow crystal (1½)
R = 166B transparent rainbow med amethyst (½)
S = 166C transparent rainbow amethyst (⅓)

TOHO SIZE 12 3-CUT BEADS
T = 82 metallic nebula (1¼)
U = 166 transparent rainbow lt amethyst (½)
V = 167BD transparent rainbow teal (¾)

TOHO 3mm BUGLE BEADS
W = 84 metallic iris green-brown (1¼)

SIZE 1 JAPANESE METAL THREAD
X = silver

KIKKO PANEL

POINTS OF INTEREST

Transparent beads in the same colour range but different finishes, threads in varied colours and different techniques are creatively combined to stitch the flowers.

The subtle differences between the flowers contribute to realising the underpinning principles of movement, texture, and dimension that is typical for Japanese embroidery.

The *kikko* pattern is a symbol of longevity based on the shell of the tortoise, which is believed to have a life span over thousands of years in folklore. The *kikko* pattern with a flower centre is referred to as a *kikko hanabishi* and is a traditional *wagara* pattern.

The arabesque design is an imported design representing spreading vines, stems, and tendrils. It was said to have been introduced into Japan from China more than two thousand years ago. The design is often combined with other patterns, especially florals, as is the case in this project.

DESIGN AND PATTERN PREPARATION

See the liftout pattern for the embroidery design.

Preparing the fabric

From the piece of teal silk cut one, 60cm x 34cm wide (23½" x 13½") and one, 73cm x 83cm wide (28¾" x 32¾"). Put the remaining silk aside for the cord ends.

On the wrong side of the smaller piece of silk, mark the fabric warp with thread or a removable fabric marker. The box panels are worked onto the smaller piece of silk and the bag top is made using the larger piece.

Transferring the design

Transfer the design referring to page 122. Three panel designs are transferred onto the smaller piece of fabric spacing them 5cm (2") apart. Mount the fabric on the frame referring to pages 123–125.

Mark in the outlines with thread using **line of held thread technique**.

FLOWER PANEL

ORDER OF WORK

Kikko panel

Kikko shape

Use the dark green sewing thread to stitch **W** and **N**. **X** is used to stitch the *kikko* lines for **H** and **P**. Thread **X** into the no. 10 sharp and knot the ends together to form a double thread for stitching.

Begin with the small rectangles and stitch three single **W** side by side in a vertical direction. Work a row of **P** around the bugle beads, beginning with the upper and lower edges with four beads then the side edges with three beads using **line of held thread – straight line technique**.

Stitch a straight line with **P** to join the corners of the rectangles using **line of**

held thread – straight line technique to complete the *kikko* shapes. Work a second line, inside the first with **N** and **W**, stitching the longer line with 1 x **N**, 3 x **W** and 1 x **N** and the short line with 1 x **N**.

Kikko flowers

Stitch the flowers with teal sewing thread.

Work a single stitch at the centre of the shape with **F** in a horizontal direction. Stitch the petals around the centre bead beginning at the cardinal points with 2 x **H** and 2 x **P**, with **H** on the outer edge. These stitches should not meet the centre bead. Work two stitches in each quarter in the same manner to complete each flower.

Flower panel

All the flowers are worked in a similar manner with variations in bead

combinations and techniques. Refer to the three panel guides for the variations. Each element is stitched in the following manner:

Stitch a single bead at the base of each flower with **A** for the small, three-petal flower and **B** for the larger flowers, aligned to the stem.

Full petals with padding

Using **raised effect – general padding technique**, work the padding using two rows for the large petals and one row for the smaller petals leaving a one bead space along the top and side edges of the petal. Stitch the petals with vertical single layer technique. Larger beads are positioned on the outer edge of the petal to taper the shape.

PANEL 1 GUIDE

FRONT PETALS
Green thread–padding **U, I, R**
BACK PETALS
Green thread–raised effect, stitch length **U, I, R**

FRONT PETALS
Green thread–padding
Centre petal: **U, L**
Side petals: **L**
BACK PETALS
White thread–raised effect,
stitch length **U, L**

FRONT PETALS
White thread **R**
BACK PETALS
Centre petal:
White thread–padding **J, R**
Side petals:
Green thread **S**

FRONT PETALS
Green thread–padding **I, R**
BACK PETALS
White thread–raised effect,
stitch length **I, S**

FRONT PETALS
Centre petal:
Green thread–padding
G, L
Side petals: Outline
with white thread **L**
BACK PETALS
Green thread **G, L**

FRONT PETALS
Centre petal: White thread–padding **R**
Side petals: Green thread **S**

FRONT PETALS Green thread–padding **I, R**
BACK PETALS Green thread–raised effect, stitch length **U, R**

PANEL 2 GUIDE

FRONT PETALS Green thread–padding
Centre petal: **U, L**
Side petals: **L**
BACK PETALS Green thread–padding **U, L**

FRONT PETALS
White thread–padding **I, R**
BACK PETALS
Green thread–raised effect,
stitch length **J, R, S**

FRONT PETALS
Green thread **S**
BACK PETALS
Green thread–padding **J, S**

FRONT PETALS
White thread–padding **U, R**
BACK PETALS
White thread–raised effect,
stitch length **U, R**

FRONT PETALS
Green thread–padding **G, L**
BACK PETALS
Centre petal:
Green thread–padding **G, L**
Side petals:
White thread **G, L**

FRONT PETALS
Centre petal: Green thread–padding **G, R**
Side petals: Green thread **S**

FRONT PETALS
Centre petal: Green thread–padding **U, R**
Side petals: Green thread–padding **U, R** Outline with white thread **U**
BACK PETALS Green thread–padding **U, R**

FRONT PETALS Green thread–padding
Centre petal: **U**, **R**
Side petals: **R**
BACK PETALS Green thread–raised effect, stitch length **U**, **S**

FRONT PETALS
White thread–padding **G**, **L**
BACK PETALS
White thread–raised effect,
stitch length **U**, **R**

FRONT PETALS
White thread–padding **I**, **R**
BACK PETALS
Green thread **I**, **R**

FRONT PETALS
White thread **R**
BACK PETALS
Centre petal:
White thread–padding **I**, **R**
Side petals:
White thread–raised effect,
stitch length **R**

FRONT PETALS
White thread–padding **G**, **L**
BACK PETALS
Green thread **G**, **L**

FRONT PETALS
Centre petal:
White thread–raised effect, stitch length **R**
Side petals: Green thread **S**

FRONT PETALS Green thread–padding
Centre petal: **U**, **R**, **L**
Side petals: **J**, **R**, **L**
BACK PETALS Green thread–raised effect, stitch length **U**, **R**, **S**

Full petals with no padding

Work the petals using **vertical single layer technique**, creating a slight raised effect where indicated with **raised effect – stitch length adjustment technique**, adding one extra bead to the stitch length.

Side view petals

Outline the underside of the petal using **couching technique 1 – combination needle-koma method**. Complete the petal **using diagonal single layer technique** beginning at the petal tip. Use right diagonal for the left-hand petals and left diagonal for the right-hand petals. Stitch the flower centre with **O** using **scatter effect technique – singles**.

Tendrils and stems

Work with **S** using **couching technique 1 – combination needle-koma method** for the longer lines and **line of held thread –** **curved line method** for the short lines.

Leaves

All leaves are stitched using **diagonal single layer technique** with **L** and **E** on the outer edge. Begin at the tip of the leaf and work to the base. If the leaf is oriented in a clockwise direction from the tip, stitch as a right diagonal. If oriented counter-clockwise from the tip, work as a left diagonal.

Background

Fill the background with **scatter effect – singles technique** with **T** and **M** in tight, tapered areas. Note that the background extends into the edges of the *kikko* panel.

Bag top

Preparing the bag top

With right sides together and matching edges, fold the larger piece of teal silk in half down the length and machine stitch with a 1cm (3⁄8") seam allowance forming a tube. Press the seam open. With right sides together and matching raw edges, fold the upper half of the tube down inside the lower half and press to create a centre foldline. Open out the fold.

With the seam on one side, finger press the fold at the opposite side for 3cm (1¼") on each side of the centre foldline. Cut the piece of lightweight fusible interfacing in half so that there are two, 5cm x 2cm wide (2" x ¾") pieces. Centre one piece of fusible interfacing over the 6cm (2⅜") fold and fuse in place. Repeat on the side with a seam. Turn to the right side. Make a 4cm (1½") buttonhole centred over the centre foldline on each fused area, working parallel to the stitched seam. With wrong sides together and matching raw edges, re-fold the fabric and re-press the centre foldline.

posh

Machine stitch a casing around the centre foldline, 13mm (½") from the fold.

Mark a 1.5cm (⅝") seam at the lower edges.

Beading

Open out the fold. Beginning at the side seam, mark lines at 4.5cm (1¾") intervals on one half of the fabric. Stitch single C, D and V along the lines, with the smaller beads at the top and the larger beads at the base, working in a random manner with the space between the beads reducing towards the base and finishing 2mm (¹⁄₁₆") from the casing. Re-fold with the beaded lines to the outside.

Machine stitch the layers together along the marked lower seamline.

CONSTRUCTION

All seam allowances are 1.5cm (⅝") unless specified.

1 Complete the finishing process referring to page 132.

2 Cut three, 9cm x 27cm wide (3½" x 10⅝") pieces of medium-weight fusible wadding, checking the size against the beaded panels. Place a towel beneath the beaded surface and fuse one piece of wadding in place on the wrong side of each beaded panel.

3 Remove the beaded fabric from the frame and cut out each panel leaving a 1.5cm (⅝") seam allowance. Pin and ladder stitch the panels together along the short edges, forming a circle.

4 With right sides together and matching raw edges, stitch the bag top to the upper edge of the panels with small slip stitches approximately 2.5mm (³⁄₃₂") apart just above the stitched seamline.

5 Using the box as a template, trace the hexagon outline onto paper twice. Trim away 4.5mm (⁵⁄₃₂") from each side on one paper template. Check the sizing against the inside of the hexagonal box. It should be a snug fit. Adjust if necessary.

6 Using the larger paper template, mark and cut out the shape from the black adhesive vinyl. Using the smaller paper template, mark and cut out the shape from the black adhesive felt. Cut

two, 9cm x 40cm wide (3½" x 15¾") pieces from the black adhesive felt.

7   Using the cut pieces, remove the paper backing and line the inner base and sides of the box with the adhesive felt.

8   Apply a thin layer of craft glue to the sides of the box with the brush and leave until almost dry.

9   Slowly ease the beaded fabric down over the sides of the box. It should be a snug fit. Ensure the bag top seam allowance is slipped down between the beaded fabric and the box sides so it is not visible. The lower beaded edge of the panels should be level with the base of the box. Press around the sides to glue in position. Allow to dry.

10   Turn the box upside down and clip the seam allowance at the lower edge of the beaded panels. Apply a thin layer of glue around the edge of the box base, fold in the seam allowance and press firmly to secure.

Allow to dry.

11   Remove the paper backing, centre the adhesive vinyl over the base, aligning the edges, and press firmly in place.

12   Make two, 85cm (33½") twisted cords using the perlé cotton or purchase cord in the desired colour. Thread one cord through the casing so that both ends emerge through the one buttonhole. Bind the thread ends together. Thread the second cord around the top of the bag through the casing so that both ends emerge through the second buttonhole. Bind the ends together.

13   Cut two, 6.5cm x 5cm wide (2½" x 2") pieces of teal silk taffeta. With right sides together and matching edges, fold and pin one piece in half down the length. Stitch the seam using a 6mm (¼") seam allowance, forming a tube. Finger press the seam open.

Turn to the right side. With wrong sides together and matching raw edges, fold the upper half of the tube down inside the lower half and finger press the fold. Leaving a 6mm (¼") seam allowance from the raw edges, using a doubled sewing thread and leaving a tail at each end, work a line of gathering around the tube. Finger press the seam allowance to the inside of the tube. Place 1cm (⅜") of the ends of one cord inside the tube and pull up the gathering thread firmly and tie off. Adjust the gathers evenly and stitch through the cord

several times with the thread tails to secure.

Divide the folded end of the tube into quarters and mark. Secure the sewing thread into the folded edge of the tube at one quarter mark. Place a small amount of fibre-fill inside the tube. Take a stitch through the folded edge at the opposite quarter mark and pull the edges together. Work a second stitch and secure the thread. Repeat with the two remaining quarter marks, forming a tulip shape.

Make the fabric end at the ends of the second cord in the same manner.

From Barbara...

What to make?

My project had to be something I would use frequently, be elegant and practical.

The concept of a workbag started to germinate. The original thought was a box-style bag but the plan evolved to become a more elaborate carry-all.

Intrigued by the traditions and designs of Japan I learned about the Japanese kikko motif.

It piqued my interest as I also enjoy English paper piecing and the shape of the kikko reminded me of hexagons and Grandma's Garden patchwork.

The concept of covering a hexagonal box for the bottom of the workbag was debated and prototypes were commissioned.

Six panels of different beading could look chaotic in my mind.

The kikko was to be a standout feature.

In discussion with Margaret, we both liked the idea of repeating 2 panels three times around the bag bottom – a kikko feature and a floral feature.

It was starting to come together.

What fabric to use?

The colour had to be rich.

Teal, purple, aqua...

I chose the beautiful blue Indian taffeta silk but it did need to be lined for the beading as it was a particularly fine fabric.

Which beads to use?

The bead choices for the kikko were the next decision to be made.

I had decided the inner lines of the kikko should be silver. However, after I started, I found the reflection difficult for my eyes. Not to be beaten, after discussion with Margaret about my difficulty, I trialled a clear AB bead with a silver metallic thread – problem solved.

Then came the defining lines of the kikko and the enclosed squares to be filled.

The blue green combos were trialled for colour and fit.

After much sampling a particular combination of bugles and seed beads proved to fit the size and shape.

It came down to a choice of two very close colours but one just sang more loudly than the other.

The flowers inside the kikko were a more difficult choice.

With much of my work with Margaret in the past I had often used different coloured threads through beads to change their appearance

Once again that knowledge came into play after auditioning many beads I decided the one that gave just the right hue was the clear AB again but with a blue thread through it changing it to a soft blue glow.

Then came the beads for the repeated floral panels...

I wanted the floral to be the same colour tones but not exact replicas.

So, it was back to sampling once again.

My leaning was towards muted colours. I easily settled on the dusty pink and purples with each of the panels using just a few colours but varying which flower the colours featured in and once again employing different thread colours to change the colour depths.

What could I do with the top section of the bag?

With such a heavily decorated base section of the workbag it seemed I must do something other than a perfectly plain silk bag at the top.

I like simplicity. Margaret mentioned that she had ordered some crystals that may match the silk colour well.

I thought, they would perhaps look good "raining" down the sides of the bag onto the panels.

With my idea of rain now in my head it was just a matter of how close together to place them.

Towards the top of the bag the beading needed to be fine, even the small crystals would be a bit heavy.

In the end the green-blue seed beads looked perfect.

How to close the bag?

I had originally wanted to make kumihimo cords for the bag.

I started sampling with eight threads of perlé 8 and didn't like the look. I doubled them and still didn't like the look so went to thirty-two strands and was happy with the cords.

Then, as I constructed the bag I drew the conclusion they were too heavy for such delicate silk.

So, back to sampling... this time sixteen strands again but using an eight-cord pattern.

Result – perfect.

What to name my project?

People kept asking me what I was working at making.

I would reply saying it was a "knitting bag". Consistently the reply to that was that it was too nice and too fancy for a knitting bag. One day I responded with, "Well it's a POSH knitting bag!" and that is how the name POSH came about.

I am super pleased to have had this opportunity to share my work.

The time I spend with Margaret as a tutor and friend is incredibly valuable to me and I do believe it shows in the finished work.

A DIFFERENT INTERPRETATION

Jacqueline Poirier stitched the alternative project from the same design. She made a hexagonal box with a lid. Jacqueline is a certified Japanese embroidery teacher as well and her work is always meticulous. Over the years of my association with Jacqueline, I have greatly appreciated the opportunity to exchange views on embroidery and see things from a different cultural perspective. This has added to my own personal development in the subject of creativity.

As Jacqueline made her project into a box, we had a separate design for the lid to complete it. This design is also included in this book for anyone who may wish to do the same. Here are Jacqueline's comments on her creative process for the project:

"Among the designs Margaret suggested, this one immediately caught my eye. The mandala spirit, more geometric than anything I'd done before, really suited me.

Starting with just a black-and-white drawing, without any photos of the work, was a real challenge. First question: what colour? I like blue, so blue and... yellow or gold?

The next step was to turn the black-and-white drawing into colour: these choices are important because they completely transform the drawing, highlighting certain shapes rather than others.

All that remained was to imagine which stitches to put where and choose the beads to realise these ideas. I chose beads from the aquamarine range for the blue and, on Margaret's advice, bronze beads for the golden yellow. For the flower in the centre and the arabesques on the edge, it seemed obvious that gold thread embroidery would be more suitable than beads.

With the strategy defined, the embroidery could begin, guided by Margaret. First the gold thread embroidery, then the pearls, starting with the centre. The process wasn't very complicated for the lid, just a few changes in the distribution of light and dark colours to highlight certain parts of the design.

All that remained was to deal with the sides. No difficulty for the flowered sides, but it took several tries to find a satisfying solution for the squared sides. The hanabishi in the center of each square are easily embroidered with thread, but it was a challenge to figure out how to embroider them with pearls while retaining their characteristics.

It was a lot of work, but how satisfying and what a pleasure to look at the finished box!"

WAU BULAN

The design for this project took root from a discussion with Razi Wight when I asked if she would like to do a project for this book and, if given a choice, what would it be. Our discussion revolved around a Malaysian theme and colours from our country of birth. Razi suggested the *wau bulan*. It is a great example of a design from a cultural source.

The *wau bulan* is a Malaysian icon and is mainly associated with the state of Kelantan. Literally translated as moon kite from its Malay name, the *wau bulan* is a large kite often spanning 2.5m (2yd 27") and standing 3.5m (3yd 30") tall. Made of a bamboo frame and brightly coloured paper, it has a distinctive crescent shape for its lower section, hence its name. The upper section has two distinct colour patches and the rest of the kite is ornately decorated. Strongly coloured floral patterns are a common theme. The strong colours make it visible in the air and the crescent shape gives the appearance of a rising crescent moon.

Coloured streamers on the outer points of the kite complete the shape.

wau bulan

POINTS OF INTEREST

The design was created so that it can be adapted for two different projects, even three. The larger part of the design can be used independently to decorate a box top. The sample project is made into an evening bag. Different colour schemes were used for the two different projects, both reminiscent of the colours of Malaysia.

Metallic paint was used for the two patches that typically adorn the kite. The two sections are intended to reflect sunlight whilst in the air so the metallic colours give this impression.

The finished bag measures
14cm x 23.5cm wide (5 ½" x 9 ¼").

Techniques Used:

*Couching technique 1 – combination
needle-koma*

Diagonal single layer

Japanese running stitch

Line of held thread – circle

Line of held thread – curved line

Line of held thread – straight line

*Line of staggered diagonals – metallic
thread*

Scatter effect technique – singles

Separated single layer

Simple multi-petal flower

Simple multi-petal flower – variation 1

*Single stitches with one and multiple
beads*

Standard leaves

Vertical single layer

Fabric and supplies

65cm x 56cm wide (25 ½" x 22") piece
of magenta silk taffeta

44cm x 24cm wide (17 ¼" x 9 ½") piece
of heavyweight fusible interlining

30cm x 20cm wide (12" x 8") piece of
medium-weight fusible interfacing

44cm x 24cm wide (17 ¼" x 9 ½") piece
of 1mm adhesive felt

50wt off-white cotton sewing thread

50wt dark magenta cotton sewing
thread

Magenta polyester sewing thread

Jacquard Lumiere metallic paint
561 gold

Posca marking pen metallic pink

Size 5 acrylic paint brush

1.5cm (⅝") magnetic bag closure

Craft glue

Needles

No. 26 chenille
No. 3 milliner's
No. 10 sharp
No. 12 sharp

Beads and thread

*Bead quantities listed refer to a
5cm x 12mm (2" x ½") tube*

CZECH 3mm FIRE-POLISHED BEADS
A = orange lamé (6 pieces)

CZECH 4mm FIRE-POLISHED BEADS
B = smoky topaz lustre (2 pieces)

PRECIOSA SIZE 9 3-CUT BEADS
C = emerald lustre (⅓)
D = red AB (¾)

PRECIOSA SIZE 12 3-CUT BEADS
E = emerald lustre (¾)
F = green lustre (½)

TOHO SIZE 11 SEED BEADS
G = 22 silver-lined lt topaz (⅛)
H = 167 transparent rainbow
peridot (⅓)
I = 174B transparent rainbow
orange (⅛)
J = 221 bronze (¼)
K = 356 inside colour lt amethyst
fuchsia-lined (6)
L = 459 gold lustre dk topaz (½)
M = 551 perma-finish galvanised rose
gold (3 pieces)
N = 557 perma-finish galvanised
starlight (10 pieces)
O = 901 Ceylon rice pudding (¼)

TOHO SIZE 15 SEED BEADS
P = 5C transparent ruby (⅛)
Q = 6C transparent amethyst (1 ½)
R = 10B transparent med orange (1/16)
S = 22 silver-lined lt topaz (¼)
T = 148 Ceylon peach cobbler (⅛)

U = 167 transparent rainbow peridot (1/16)
V = 221 bronze (1/16)
W = 459 gold lustre dk topaz (¼)
X = 551 perma-finish galvanised rose
gold (20 pieces)
Y = 569 perma-finish galvanised teal (⅛)
Z = 2110 silver-lined milky lt topaz (1 ¼)

TOHO SIZE 12 3-CUT BEADS
AA = 103 transparent lustre
lt topaz (⅓)
AB = 932 inside colour aqua
Capri-lined (12 pieces)

TOHO 3mm BUGLE BEADS
AC = 5 transparent lt Siam ruby (1 ½)

SIZE 1 JAPANESE METAL THREAD
AD = multi-colour gold

DESIGN AND PATTERN PREPARATION

See the liftout pattern for the embroidery design.

Preparing the fabric

Cut a piece, 46cm x 29cm wide (18⅛" x 11½") from the magenta silk taffeta.

Cut a 19cm x 28cm wide (7½" x 11") piece of magenta silk taffeta for the gussets.

On the wrong side, mark the fabric warp with thread or a removable fabric marker.

The remaining fabric is used for the bag and gusset linings.

Transferring the design

Transfer the design referring to page 122. Mount the fabrics on separate frames referring to pages 123–125.

Mark in the outline and darts on each fabric with thread using **line of held thread technique** for straight sections and *Japanese running stitch* for curved sections.

Colouring and gilding the fabric

Using the metallic gold paint and paint brush, gild the top of the pot, the small oval shape between the two, patterned sections and the two, large, fancy shapes in the larger patterned section ensuring there is good coverage. Colour the centre of the cream, oval flowers with the metallic pink marking pen.

ORDER OF WORK

When using **AD**, half-hitch the thread onto the needle to form a double thread.

Main outlines

Work an outline around the two large sections with **Q** using *couching technique 1 – combination needle-koma method*. Add a second outline outside the first with **AC** and the dark magenta sewing thread. On the inner edge of the first outline work diagonal stitches with 2 x **Z**. Begin with a vertical stitch at the midpoint of each shape and work right diagonal stitches to the right-hand side and left diagonal stitches to the left-hand side.

Stitch the line joining the two, large shapes with **G** using *couching technique 1 – combination needle-koma method*. Outline the gilded oval with **J** using the same technique.

Large oval shape

Centre flower

Stitch a single **A** at the centre aligned horizontally across the design. Encircle with **Q** using *line of held thread – circle method*. Stitch petals as for *simple multi-petal flower* with **S** and **AA**, using at least three **AA** on the outer edge of each stitch. Work the red petals as for *standard leaves* with **V** for the vein and **P** and **D** for the outer section. Stitch the gold leaves in a similar manner with **AA** and **S**. Work the centre vein with **AD** using *line of staggered diagonals – metallic thread*.

Gold leaf shapes

Outline each shape with **L**, tapering at the indents to **W** with *couching technique 1 – combination needle-koma method*. Stitch the lines of foliage with **E** using *couching technique 1 – combination needle-koma method* for longer lines and *line of held thread – curved line method* for short lines. Add single, spaced stitches at the centre with **V**, **J** and **B**, tapering at each end.

Stems and veins

Work all the leaf veins and twining stems with **AD** half-hitched onto the needle to create a double thread using *line of staggered diagonals – metallic thread*. Refer to Stitch Direction Guide A for use of left and right diagonals.

Floral motifs

Stitch the motifs at the north and south points of the red flower in the following manner:

Work the curved tendrils with **W** and stitch a single **A** and **I** and/or **R** within the shape.

Stitch the leaves using diagonal single layer technique for those without veins or as standard leaves for those with veins using **AA** and **S** for the gold leaves, **H** and **U** for the green leaves and **I** and **R** for the orange leaves.

Work the motifs at the tips of the gold leaf shapes in a similar manner. Stitch the curved tendrils with **W**, adding perpendicular stitches with 2–3 x **W** and stitch a single **A**, **I** and **R** within the shape. Use **C** and **E** for the leaves on the centre tendrils and **S** and **AA** for the gold leaves.

Red flowers

Stitch as *simple multi-petal flower – variation 1* with 1 x **N** for the centre and 2 x **D** and 1 x **P** for each petal.

Cream flowers

Stitch as *simple multi-petal flower – variation 1* with 1 x **AB** at the centre and 1 x **O** and 2 x **T** for each petal, working in an oval shape and leaving a negative space of 1–1½ beads around the centre bead.

Leaves

Stitch the leaves using diagonal single layer technique for those without veins or as standard leaves for those with veins

RIGHT DIAGONAL   RIGHT DIAGONAL   LEFT DIAGONAL   LEFT DIAGONAL

LEFT DIAGONAL   LEFT DIAGONAL   RIGHT DIAGONAL   RIGHT DIAGONAL

STITCH DIRECTION GUIDE A – Line of Staggered Diagonals

using **AA** and **S** for the gold leaves, **H** and **U** for the green leaves, **I** and **R** for the orange leaves and **F** for those leaves marked with X on Stitch Direction Guide A. Add single **Y** as marked along the stems.

Background

Fill the background using *scatter effect technique – singles* with **Q** and dark magenta sewing thread.

Large crescent shape

Urn

Outline the upper edge of the urn with **AD** using *line of staggered diagonals – metallic thread*. Stitch the parallel lines at the neck with **X** for the upper line and **X** and 2 x **M** at the centre for the lower line using *line of held thread – straight*

line technique. Work the upper section with **J** and **V** using *vertical single layer technique*, beginning with the centre stitch. Increase the number of **V** as required as the stitches are worked outwards.

Stitch the lower section in the same manner, fanning the stitches from the neck. Complete the leaves and stems emanating from the urn in the same manner as the floral motifs on the oval shape.

Red flowers

Variation 1

Stitch a single **N** at the base of the flower. Add single stitches for petals with **D** tapering at each end with **P** and working the centre stitch first and alternating side stitches. Tie down to shape.

Variation 2

Stitch the petals first beginning with the centre stitch then working the side stitches with **D** tapering at each end with **P**. Add 3 x **Y** at the centre and work random stitches with **AD** to form stamens.

Stems, leaves and cream flowers

Work all the leaf veins and twining stems with **AD** using *line of staggered diagonals – metallic thread*. Refer to Stitch Direction Guide B for the use of left and right diagonals. Work the leaves and cream flowers in the same manner as those on the large oval shape, with **F** for those leaves marked with X on Stitch Direction Guide B.

Background

Fill the background using *scatter effect technique – singles* with **Q**.

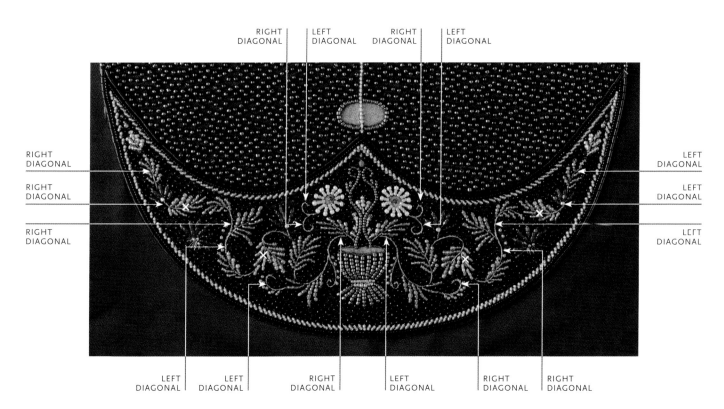

STITCH DIRECTION GUIDE B – Line of Staggered Diagonals

Main background

Check that the marked position for the magnetic closure remains centred and mark out the size of the closure. Do not place any beads within the marked area. The remaining background area is filled with **K** using *scatter effect technique – singles*.

It is important that the size of the beaded area is squared exactly so the background is worked in two stages.

Begin filling the background from the centre of the design, working out towards the edges. Do not stitch beyond the edge of the motifs at this stage. Re-measure the marked outline to ensure that the length and width remain accurate and adjust if necessary.

Complete filling the background right to the edge of the marked area.

Gusset

Work a row of beads along the top edge of each gusset shape with **K** using *line of held thread – straight line technique*. Stitch single beads spaced one bead apart around the inside edge of the remaining outline. Fill with **K** using *scatter effect technique – singles*, taking care to ensure the beads are spaced 2mm (¹⁄₁₆") apart, face different directions and don't form lines.

CONSTRUCTION

*All seam allowances are 1.5cm (⁵⁄₈")
unless specified.*

1 Complete the finishing process referring to page 132.

2 Using the black pen, transfer the template shaping to tracing paper and cut out. Pin the template to the felt and cut out, 2mm (¹⁄₁₆") smaller than the template all around.

3 Place the beaded fabric in the frame, wrong side uppermost, onto a towel over a hard surface. Peel away the backing paper and position the felt, adhesive side down, over the wrong side of the embroidery and press gently. Check to ensure that the felt is positioned correctly. The stitching marking the outline should be visible outside the felt.

Apply pressure to the felt in a sweeping motion from the centre outwards to ensure it is securely attached. Remove the fabric from the frame and cut out leaving a 1.5cm (⁵⁄₈") seam allowance. Clip the rounded ends. Apply a thin layer of craft glue to the edge of the seam allowance only. Fold under the seam allowance and glue in position. The outer line of beads should be visible. Fit half the magnetic closure in position.

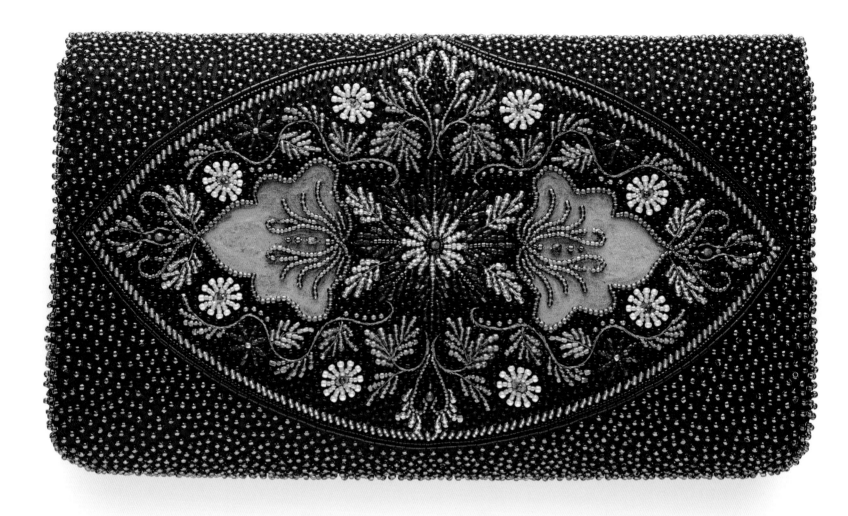

4. Cut out the heavyweight fusible interlining using the bag lining template and fuse to the wrong side of the lining fabric. Adding a 1.5cm (⅝") seam allowance, cut out the lining.

   Apply a thin layer of craft glue to the edge of the seam allowance only. Fold under the seam allowance and glue in position.

5. Using the bag gusset template, cut four pieces of medium-weight fusible interfacing. Fuse one piece to the wrong side of each beaded gusset. Remove the gusset fabric from the frame and cut out each gusset leaving a 1cm (⅜") seam allowance. Stitch the darts and clip the rounded edges. Prepare the gusset linings in the same manner using the remaining pieces of fusible interfacing. With

wrong sides facing and matching edges, slip stitch each lining piece to a beaded gusset piece.

6. Align the beaded fabric and lining at the squared edge and slip stitch the bag and lining together along the short edge and long straight edges for 29cm (11½") from the right-angle corner on each side.

7. Attach the gussets to the lined bag piece with ladder stitch and the polyester thread. Begin at the dart and work up one side to the upper edge, ensuring the top end finishes exactly at the opening corner. At the end, re-stitch for 1cm (⅜") to reinforce.

   Return to the dart and stitch the second side in place in the same manner. Use clips to hold the pieces together while stitching to prevent slipping. Repeat to attach the second gusset.

8. Position and hold the lining and beaded bag together with a clip at the centre of the curved edge. Fold the flap over the bag and position the remaining half of the magnetic closure on the lining. Secure in place. Holding the flap and lining together in a curved position as if closing the bag, ladder stitch up one side and then the other. Hold the edges together with clips while stitching to ensure that the precise positioning is maintained.

9. Fill the bag with acid-free tissue paper to hold the shape and steam, paying particular attention to the gussets and flap foldover. Finger press as necessary to shape. Remove the tissue paper and replace with fresh. Leave the bag to dry overnight.

A DIFFERENT INTERPRETATION

The framed picture is stitched by Razi Wight in an alternative colour scheme. The outline of the kite was done with a different technique that more accurately replicates that of a moon kite. It was not however, practically suitable for a bag.

Here is what she has to say about her project.

"I felt very honoured to be asked if I would like to do a project for this book.

In discussion with Margaret, we finalised the idea of the wau bulan, which is one of Malaysia's national symbols. I chose the traditional colours of the batik fabric used in traditional Malay garments. It was a big challenge for me.

It was also very exciting. As I started the embroidery, I could see the colours blossom and the pattern coming to life.

The project was originally to be made into a notebook cover. As the embroidery progressed, I felt it was not going to do it justice, so I changed my mind and decided to make it as a box top.

Well, that did not look right either because of the tassels. When I finished it was obvious it had to be framed upright to appreciate the beauty of the kite."

GARDEN SYMPHONY

Inspired by Jacobean-era patterns, the leaves in this design are given equal prominence to the flowers for a colourful display.

Garden Symphony is designed with a degree of challenge to the embroiderer who is required to make interpretive decisions on the number and combination of bead colours and size in each stitch to create colour shading. A great project to consolidate techniques and design ideas and reinforce the three pillars of Nuido.

POINTS OF INTEREST

The ground fabric used in this project is a deep navy. This dark colour will have a strong bearing on any transparent beads used, especially light-coloured ones. Borrowing from the traditional *Yuzen* dyeing style, all the design elements are coloured. This serves to enrich the bead colours and complement the bead embroidery techniques used.

Some of the larger leaf shapes are uncommon and require some planning and considered decisions on technique selection to create good visual impressions within the design.

While the large leaves are prominent, there are numerous small leaves as well.

Different size beads are used to create form.

The small leaves are stitched in different ways with different colour combinations to create linear dimension and visual interest.

garden symphony

The finished folio measures
26.5cm x 19.5cm wide (10 ½" x 7 ¾").

Techniques Used:

*Couching technique 1 – combination
needle-koma*

Diagonal single layer

Japanese running stitch

Line of held thread – straight line

Line of held thread – curved line

Long and short stitch

Raised effect – general padding

Raised effect – outline padding

Raised effect – stitch length adjustment

Scatter effect technique – singles

Separated single layer

*Single stitches with one and
multiple beads*

Straight stitch

Vertical single layer

Fabric and supplies

20cm x 30cm wide (8" x 12") piece
of dark blue silk taffeta

27cm x 16cm wide (10 ½" x 6 ¼")
piece of 1mm adhesive felt

A5 folio frame with zip

50wt aqua cotton sewing thread

50wt black cotton sewing thread

50wt lt sapphire blue sewing thread

50wt white cotton sewing thread

12wt black *Wonderfil* Egyptian
cotton thread

Jacquard Lumiere metallic paint
561 gold

Jacquard Lumiere metallic paint
562 olive green

Jacquard Lumiere metallic paint 571
pearlescent turquoise

Jacquard Lumiere metallic paint 572
pearlescent emerald

Pebeo setacolor fabric paint opaque
raspberry

Pebeo setacolor fabric paint
opaque red

Pebeo setacolor fabric paint shimmer
opaque pearl

Posca marking pen metallic violet

Posca marking pen blue

Size 3 acrylic paint brush

Size 5 acrylic paint brush

Craft glue

Needles

No. 3 milliner's
No. 11 sharp
No. 12 sharp

Beads and thread

*Bead quantities listed refer to a
5cm x 12mm (2" x ½") tube*

CZECH 4mm FIRE-POLISHED BEADS
A = green iris (1 piece)

PRECIOSA SIZE 9 3-CUT BEADS
B = aqua lustre (⅔)
C = red AB (½)
D = ruby lustre (⅓)

PRECIOSA SIZE 12 3-CUT BEADS
E = green iris (⅓)
F = green lustre (¼)
G = red (1/16)
H = red AB (⅓)
I = ruby lustre (¼)

TOHO SIZE 8 SEED BEADS
J = 22 silver-lined lt topaz (10 pieces)

TOHO SIZE 11 SEED BEADS
K = 1 transparent crystal (¼)
L = 13 transparent lt sapphire (⅓)
M = 22 silver-lined lt topaz (¼)
N = 35 silver-lined sapphire (⅛)
O = 87 transparent rainbow cobalt (½)
P = 108 transparent lustre peridot (⅛)
Q = 165B transparent rainbow Siam
ruby (⅓)
R = 167 transparent rainbow
peridot (⅓)
S = 168 transparent rainbow lt
sapphire (⅓)
T = 174B transparent rainbow med
orange (½)
U = 178 transparent rainbow
sapphire (⅓)
V = 192 inside colour crystal yellow-
lined (¼)
W = 241 inside colour rainbow lt topaz
mauve-lined (⅛)

X = 341 inside colour crystal tomato-lined (¼)

Y = 377 inside colour lt sapphire metallic teal-lined (1)

Z = 779 inside colour rainbow crystal salmon-lined (⅓)

AA = 928 inside colour rainbow rosaline opaque purple-lined (⅓)

TOHO SIZE 15 SEED BEADS

AB = 1 transparent crystal (¼)

AC = 3B transparent dk aquamarine (⅛)

AD = 5C transparent ruby (20 pieces)

AE = 6 transparent lt amethyst (⅛)

AF = 7BD transparent Capri blue (⅛)

AG = 10B transparent med orange (⅛)

AH = 13 transparent lt sapphire (¼)

AI = 22 silver-lined lt topaz (¼)

AJ = 28 silver-lined cobalt (⅓)

AK = 49 opaque jet (¼)

AL = 87 transparent rainbow cobalt (¼)

AM = 108 transparent lustre peridot (⅓)

AN = 161 transparent rainbow crystal (⅛)

AO = 162B transparent rainbow med topaz (⅛)

AP = 162C transparent rainbow topaz (¼)

AQ = 167 transparent rainbow peridot (⅓)

AR = 168 transparent rainbow lt sapphire (⅛)

AS = 178 transparent rainbow sapphire (⅛)

AT = 241 inside colour rainbow lt topaz mauve-lined (⅛)

AU = 264 inside colour rainbow crystal teal-lined (⅛)

AV = 290 transparent lustre rose (⅓)

AW = 332 gold lustre raspberry (¼)

AX = 779 inside colour rainbow crystal salmon-lined (⅓)

AY = 928 inside colour rainbow rosaline opaque purple-lined (⅛)

TOHO SIZE 12 3-CUT BEADS

AZ = 49 opaque jet (2 ¼)

BA = 101 transparent lustre crystal (⅓)

BB = 103 transparent lustre lt topaz (⅓)

BC = 108 transparent lustre peridot (¼)

BD = 290 transparent lustre rose (⅓)

BE = 332 gold lustre raspberry (¼)

TOHO SIZE 15 3-CUT BEADS

BF = 101 transparent lustre crystal (1/16)

BG = 108 transparent lustre peridot (¼)

SIZE 1 JAPANESE METAL THREAD

BH = gold

DESIGN AND PATTERN PREPARATION

See the liftout pattern for the embroidery design.

Preparing the fabric

On the wrong side, mark the fabric warp with thread or a removable fabric marker.

Transferring the design

Transfer the design referring to page 122.

Mount the fabric on the frame referring to pages 123–125. Mark in the outline with thread using **line of held thread technique** for straight sections and **Japanese running stitch** for curved sections.

Painting and gilding the fabric

Apply the colour and gilding before commencing the embroidery using the photograph as a guide. Paint colours can be mixed to produce different results.

Before applying *Jacquard Lumiere* colours 562, 571 and 572, apply a layer of *Pebeo setacolor* shimmer opaque pearl to the relevant areas and allow to dry. Once the painting is complete, iron to set the paint following the manufacturer's instructions.

FLOWER 3

FLOWER 6 v1

FLOWER 5

FLOWER 9

FLOWER 1 v1

FLOWER 6 v2

FLOWER 8

FLOWER 4

FLOWER 6 v2

FLOWER 2

FLOWER 7

ORDER OF WORK

Flowers, berries and stems

Flower 1

The flower has three groups of petals – outer, middle and inner. The middle petals are foreground to the others and should be stitched first. All petals are stitched from the tip to the base.

Middle petals

Work the petals using **vertical single layer technique** with **AV, BD, C** and **H**. Begin with a stitch down the centre of the petal. Work stitches alternately on each side until the petal is complete. Beads are used in the order listed. Adjust the number of beads for each colour and size as necessary and tie down to shape.

Outer petals

Stitch the petals using **long and short stitch technique** combined with **raised effect – outline padding technique** with **C, BD, AV** and **H** for the surface stitching and **AB** for the padding.

Couch a line of padding along the outer edge of the petal with **AB** using **line of held thread – curved line method**. The padding begins and ends one bead space in from the design line and edges on each side.

Begin surface stitching with a stitch down the petal centre. Work **long and short stitch technique** alternately on each side following the contours of the petal. **C** is used for the first row with 1–2 **H** to taper as necessary. **H** is also used to work the outermost stitches to taper and complete the shape. **BD** and **AV** are used for the second and subsequent row with

AV positioned towards the centre of the flower.

Inner petals

Stitch the petals using **vertical single layer technique** with **raised effect – stitch length adjustment method** with **AI, BB** and **AN**. Each petal is worked with three stitches with only the centre stitch raised by adding 1–2 beads. Work from the tip to the base. Beads are used in the listed sequence with 2 x **AI** at the tip and adjusting the number of **BB** and **AN** as necessary for the stitch length and colour.

Work the stamens, using **BH** half-hitched on the needle to form a double thread for the straight stitch filaments, and adding anthers with single **J** and **M**.

Flower 2

This flower is worked in a similar manner to flower 1 and the outer petals are not padded.

Middle petals

Work with **AX, X, D** and **H**.

Outer petals

Work with **D, H, X, AX** and **AV**.

---

*NOTE: Always use 1–2 **AV** as the last beads of the last stitches to create the illusion of negative space between the middle and outer petals.*

Inner petals

Work with **AI** and **AN**.

Flower 3

This flower has outer and inner petals. Refer to the flower 3 guide on page 114 for bead placement. Depending on individual stitching, numbers may need to be adjusted.

Outer petals

Stitch each petal using **long and short stitch technique** combined with **scatter effect technique – singles** and **couching technique 1 – combination needle-koma method**.

Centre petal

Begin with a stitch down the centre of the petal using **raised effect – stitch length adjustment method**. This stitch extends approximately ⅔ down the petal. Tie down two beads from the end. Add a short stitch on each side making each one as long as is permitted by the contour lines.

Complete the petal with a stitch on each side, extending to the base of the petal using **couching technique 1 – combination needle-koma method**. Use **AV, AX, Z, W, AT** and **D**. Complete the petal with **D** and **I** in the remaining space using **scatter effect technique – singles**.

Side petals

The side petals are worked in the same manner as the centre petal with the following exceptions:

a All stitches lie flat on the fabric and the outermost stitch on the outer edge extends to the base of the petal and is worked using **couching technique 1 – combination needle-koma method**.

b Beads are used in the following sequence – **BD, AV, AX, W, D** and **I**. Adjust the number of beads as required for colour and shape.

Inner petals

Work in the same manner as flower 1 using **AI** and **AN**.

Calyx

Stitch each sepal in the same manner as leaves (Variation P1) using *vertical single layer with raised effect method*. Use **AQ** with **AI** at the tip and **R** for tapering and shaping.

Flower 4

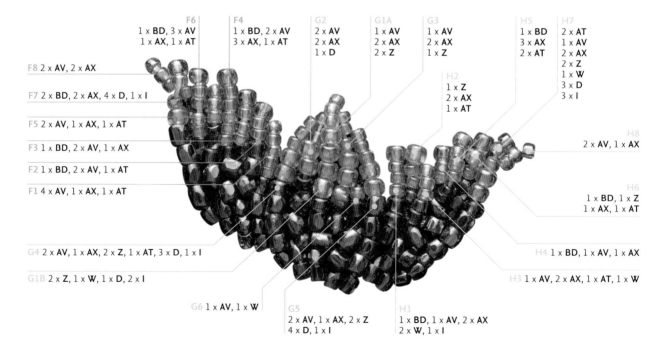

This flower has outer and inner petals. Refer to the flower 4 guides on page 115 for bead placement. Depending on individual stitching, numbers may need to be adjusted.

Sepal

Work a vertical padding stitch with three

AH positioned in the centre of the shape. Work three stitches using *vertical layer technique* to fill the shape and cover the padding stitch, ensuring neat points are achieved at each end.

Use 2 x **AH**, **S**, and 3 x **AS**, varying the number of **S** according to the stitch length. Tie down the outer stitches to shape.

Petals

All petals are worked using *vertical single layer technique* following the contours of the petals. Use **AI**, **C**, **H**, **I** and **AD** in the listed sequence, omitting **C** where the shape tapers towards the outer edge of the petal or at the base of petals, and using **AD** only as necessary to taper stitches.

Work the inner and outer petals in a similar manner to the middle petals of flower 1.

Stitch the blue petal at the centre top with three straight vertical stitches using

2 x **AJ** and 1–2 x **AH**. Fill the remaining area with **AJ** using *scatter effect technique – singles*.

Small green leaves

The leaves are worked using *vertical single layer technique* or *diagonal single layer technique* with **E** and **AI**. Begin the leaves worked with *diagonal single layer technique* with the centre stitch followed by the stitch from the tip then the stitch at the base. The first two stitches are tipped with **AI**. Work the leaves using *vertical single layer technique* with three stitches, except the partial leaf to the right of the tip that is worked with two stitches. The centre stitch of each leaf is worked as a raised stitch, adding two beads to the stitch length and tipping the stitch with 2–3 x **AI**. The stitch on each side is flat and is tied down to shape with 1–2 x **AI** at the tip. Work the leaf stem with **AC** using *line of held thread – curved line method* and the aqua sewing thread.

FLOWER 3 BEAD GUIDE

Note: All beads listed for G1A & G1B are in one stitch. The stitch is tied down at the end of G1A creating a raised effect for the top half of the stitch only.

Bead guide labels:

- **F6** 1 x **BD**, 3 x **AV** / 1 x **AX**, 1 x **AT**
- **F4** 1 x **BD**, 2 x **AV** / 3 x **AX**, 1 x **AT**
- **G2** 2 x **AV** / 2 x **AX** / 1 x **D**
- **G1A** 1 x **AV** / 2 x **AX** / 2 x **Z**
- **G3** 1 x **AV** / 2 x **AX** / 1 x **Z**
- **H5** 1 x **BD** / 3 x **AX** / 2 x **AT**
- **H7** 2 x **AT** / 1 x **AV** / 2 x **AX** / 2 x **Z** / 1 x **W** / 3 x **D** / 3 x **I**
- **F8** 2 x **AV**, 2 x **AX**
- **F7** 2 x **BD**, 2 x **AX**, 4 x **D**, 1 x **I**
- **F5** 2 x **AV**, 1 x **AX**, 1 x **AT**
- **F3** 1 x **BD**, 2 x **AV**, 1 x **AX**
- **F2** 1 x **BD**, 2 x **AV**, 1 x **AT**
- **F1** 4 x **AV**, 1 x **AX**, 1 x **AT**
- **H2** 1 x **Z** / 2 x **AX** / 1 x **AT**
- **H8** 2 x **AV**, 1 x **AX**
- **H6** 1 x **BD**, 1 x **Z** / 1 x **AX**, 1 x **AT**
- **G4** 2 x **AV**, 1 x **AX**, 2 x **Z**, 1 x **AT**, 3 x **D**, 1 x **I**
- **G1B** 2 x **Z**, 1 x **W**, 1 x **D**, 2 x **I**
- **H4** 1 x **BD**, 1 x **AV**, 1 x **AX**
- **H3** 1 x **AV**, 2 x **AX**, 1 x **AT**, 1 x **W**
- **G6** 1 x **AV**, 1 x **W**
- **G5** 2 x **AV**, 1 x **AX**, 2 x **Z** / 4 x **D**, 1 x **I**
- **H1** 1 x **BD**, 1 x **AV**, 2 x **AX** / 2 x **W**, 1 x **I**

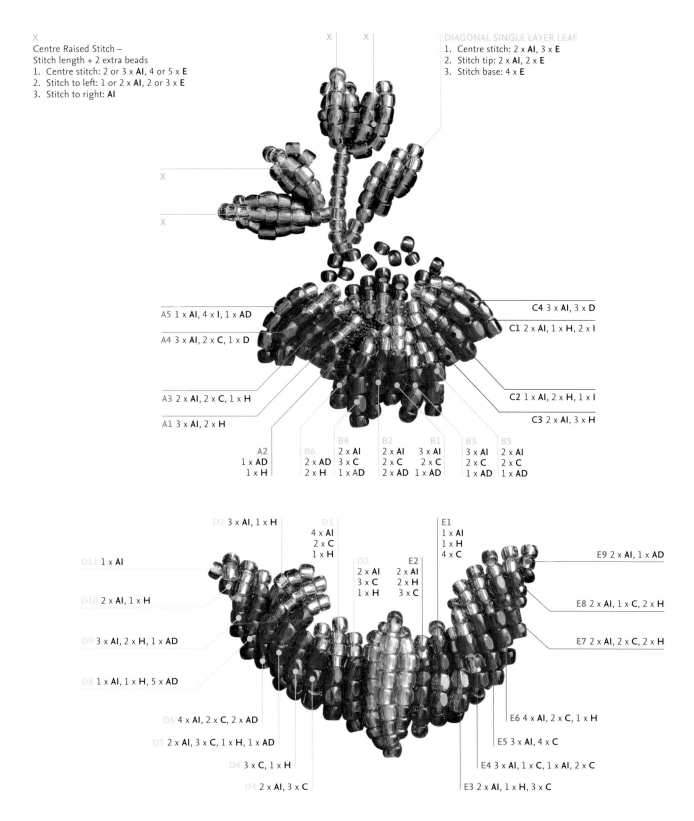

X
Centre Raised Stitch –
Stitch length + 2 extra beads
1. Centre stitch: 2 or 3 x **AI**, 4 or 5 x **E**
2. Stitch to left: 1 or 2 x **AI**, 2 or 3 x **E**
3. Stitch to right: **AI**

DIAGONAL SINGLE LAYER LEAF
1. Centre stitch: 2 x **AI**, 3 x **E**
2. Stitch tip: 2 x **AI**, 2 x **E**
3. Stitch base: 4 x **E**

A5 1 x **AI**, 4 x **I**, 1 x **AD**

A4 3 x **AI**, 2 x **C**, 1 x **D**

A3 2 x **AI**, 2 x **C**, 1 x **H**

A1 3 x **AI**, 2 x **H**

C4 3 x **AI**, 3 x **D**

C1 2 x **AI**, 1 x **H**, 2 x **I**

C2 1 x **AI**, 2 x **H**, 1 x **I**

C3 2 x **AI**, 3 x **H**

A2
1 x **AD**
1 x **H**

B6
2 x **AD**
2 x **H**

B4
2 x **AI**
3 x **C**
2 x **H**

B2
2 x **AI**
2 x **C**
2 x **AD**

B1
3 x **AI**
2 x **C**
1 x **AD**

B3
3 x **AI**
2 x **C**
1 x **AD**

B5
2 x **AI**
2 x **C**
1 x **AD**

D7 3 x **AI**, 1 x **H**

D11 1 x **AI**

D10 2 x **AI**, 1 x **H**

D9 3 x **AI**, 2 x **H**, 1 x **AD**

D8 1 x **AI**, 1 x **H**, 5 x **AD**

D6 4 x **AI**, 2 x **C**, 2 x **AD**

D5 2 x **AI**, 3 x **C**, 1 x **H**, 1 x **AD**

D4 3 x **C**, 1 x **H**

D3 2 x **AI**, 3 x **C**

D1
4 x **AI**
2 x **C**
1 x **H**

D2
2 x **AI**
3 x **C**
1 x **H**

E2
2 x **AI**
2 x **H**
3 x **C**

E1
1 x **AI**
1 x **H**
4 x **C**

E9 2 x **AI**, 1 x **AD**

E8 2 x **AI**, 1 x **C**, 2 x **H**

E7 2 x **AI**, 2 x **C**, 2 x **H**

E6 4 x **AI**, 2 x **C**, 1 x **H**

E5 3 x **AI**, 4 x **C**

E4 3 x **AI**, 1 x **C**, 1 x **AI**, 2 x **C**

E3 2 x **AI**, 1 x **H**, 3 x **C**

FLOWER 4 BEAD GUIDES

Flower 5

This flower has many layers and is stitched in sequence from foreground to background.

Calyx

Stitch a single **A** at the top of the stem. Work an arc of **AI** around the upper section of the **A** bead. Once the blue petals have been worked, stitch the upper line of each sepal with **BG** using *couching technique 1 – combination needle-koma method*. Complete with left and right diagonal stitches, ensuring they flow with the curve of the sepal.

Blue petals

Work the petals with *vertical single layer technique* with *raised effect – general padding*. Use **AS**, **N**, and **AJ** with **AS** at the tip.

Pad each petal with two rows of horizontal single beads, beginning with the centre petal and using **AS**.

Complete each petal with three stitches, working the centre one first. Tie down the centre stitch with a single couching stitch in the middle, taking care to tension the stitch so that the raised effect is not distorted. Tie down the side stitches to shape the petals. Ensure neat points are achieved with accurate stitch placement.

Centre dome-shaped petal

Stitch the inner red line with two stitches using **D** and *line of held thread – curved line method*, ensuring a neat point is achieved at the tip. Work stitches with *separated single layer technique* around the shape using **BB** and **AO**, beginning with the centre line at the tip and working down one side then the other. Fill the shape inside the red lines with **AV** using *scatter effect technique – singles.*

Outer side petals

Identify the contour lines for these petals. Work the first row with **H** and **Q** using *long and short stitch technique* and following the petal contours. Complete the petals with rows of *long and short stitch technique* using the same beads and **H** to taper the stitches.

Middle petals

Work the petals with *vertical single layer technique with raised effect* using variations for selected petals.

Variation 1

This variation applies to the two largest petals.

Pad the petals with 4 x **AT** using *general padding technique*. Work the petals with **H**, **Q**, **X** and **AV** in the listed sequence using *vertical single layer technique*. Adjust the number of beads in each line as necessary to achieve colour shading and shape.

Variation 2

Stitch the larger of the remaining petals with this variation. Pad the petal with a single stitch using 3 x **AV** in a vertical direction down the centre beginning one bead from the tip. Work the petal with **AG**, **C** and **G** in the listed sequence using *vertical single layer technique*, adjusting the number of beads in each line as necessary to achieve colour shading and shape.

Variation 3

The remaining petals are stitched using this variation using the same beads as variation 2. Work the petals using *vertical single layer technique* creating a slightly raised effect in the centre stitches using *stitch length adjustment technique*. Adjust the number of beads in each line as necessary to achieve colour shading and shape.

Flower 6

Centre

There are two variations used with the first creating a more prominent centre.

AB is used for the padding, **AE**, **AA** and **AY** are used for the purple section and **AI**, **P** and **BG** are used for the green section.

Variation 1

The purple and green sections are stitched as one using *vertical single layer technique* with a small adjustment in the stitch sequence.

Stitch the padding with **AB** using horizontal stitches ¾ down the shape stopping one bead space from the edge. Work the lines that include the green sections then the green sections that fall outside the purple sections. Fill between these stitches, omitting the green beads using *vertical single layer technique*. Tie down the outermost stitches to shape. Add single **AI** beads at the tip using *scatter effect technique – singles*, varying the number of beads according to the size of the shape.

Variation 2

The purple and green sections are stitched separately using the same beads. Work the green stitches first and tie down to shape. Stitch the horizontal padding stopping one bead space from the green section. Fill between the green sections to complete the shape using *vertical single layer technique*. Tie down the outer stitches to shape.

Outer petals

The petals are worked using **AI**, **AG**, **T** and **H** in the listed sequence with a combination of raised effect and flat stitches to create dimension.

Raised petals are worked with *raised effect – general padding* or *stitch length adjustment technique* using the following variations.

a Vertical padding – use this method for the most prominent petals. Padding is worked as a single vertical stitch with **AG** down the centre of the petal, beginning and ending 2mm (¹⁄₁₆") from each end.

b Horizontal padding – use this method to create petals that taper on the inner edge. Add 1–2 stitches with **AG** to the upper half of the petal.

c Stitch length adjustment – this method is used to raise only the centre vertical stitch. Add two extra size 15 beads to the stitch and pin stitch back under the stitch.

All petals are worked using vertical single layer technique, as necessary to achieve colour shading and shape.

Flower 7

Calyx

Stitch the centre sepal first with **AS**, **N** and **AJ** in the sequence listed using *vertical single layer technique*. Work the middle stitch of the sepal first, using *raised effect – stitch length adjustment method*. Add a stitch on each side, ensuring neat points with accurate stitch placement. Tie down to shape.

Work the sepal at each side using the same beads and *line of held thread – curved line method*.

Petals

Stitch the petals with *vertical single layer technique*, following the contour lines in a similar manner to the outer petals of flower 4. Use **I**, **D**, **W**, **AT** and **AH** in

the sequence listed using **W** and **AT** sparingly. Adjust as necessary to achieve colour shading and shape. Tie down stitches to shape as required and fill any remaining space with **AJ** using *scatter effect technique – singles*.

Stamens

Work the stamens with **AI** using *scatter effect technique – singles*.

Flower 8

Calyx

Both sepals are stitched with *diagonal single layer technique*, working the right-hand sepal with a left diagonal and the left-hand sepal with a right diagonal. Begin stitching from the tip of the sepal. Use **AH** and **AS** on the outer edge of each stitch.

Centre

Fill the centre with three stitches using *vertical single layer technique* ensuring neat points with accurate stitch placement. Work the centre stitch using *raised effect – stitch length adjustment technique*. Use **BE** with **AW** at each end to taper.

Stamens

Use **AI**, **AO** and **AP**. Work stitches radiating around the centre using *separated single layer technique* with one **AI** and **AP** at each end of each stitch, varying the number of **AO** beads as required.

Flower 9

Calyx

Outline each sepal with two stitches using **BG**, ensuring neat points with

accurate stitch placement. Fill the centre of each sepal with a single stitch using **AS** and tie down all stitches to shape.

Petals

Work the foreground centre petal first. Pad the petal with **AB** using *raised effect – general padding technique* ⅔ down the petal and leaving one bead space along the side edges. Work the petal with **I**, **D** and **AH** in the sequence listed using *vertical single layer technique*.

Stitch the remaining petals with the same beads using *vertical single layer technique*, tied down to the contour lines of each petal.

Stamens

Work the stamens with **AI** using *scatter effect technique – singles*.

Yellow flowers

The flowers have five overlapping petals and a distinct centre.

Centre

Stitch the centre on each flower with a simple 5–6-petal flower, using 5 x size 9 beads or 6 x size 15 beads.

Blue centre – use **V** for the centre and **AJ** for the petals

Red centre – use **M** for the centre and **C** or **D** for the petals.

Petals

Use **BB** and **AP** for blue-centre flowers and **BB**, **AI** and **AO** for red-centre flowers. Work each petal separately using *vertical single layer technique*. Begin with a single vertical stitch down the centre of each petal using **BB** and **AI** for the larger flowers and **BB** and **AP** for the smaller flowers. Working from the foreground to the background, complete each petal with vertical stitches using **BB** and **AO** for the large flowers and **BB** and **AP** for the small flowers, taking care to maintain the petal shape. All stitches should be angled towards the centre bead. Tuck the two outer petal stitches slightly under the adjacent stitch to round the petal. Tie down stitches to shape.

Large yellow bud

Work three raised stitches using *raised effect – stitch length adjustment technique* with **AI**, **AP** and 2 x **F**, radiating the stitches one stitch in from the design line on each side. Add two outer stitches with **AI**, **AP** and 1 x **F**. Add two stitches between the raised stitches, angling them towards the centre of the flower using the same beads. Tie down the last four stitches to shape.

Large red bud

Work three raised stitches using *raised effect – stitch length adjustment technique* with 1 x **H**, 2 x **AP** and 1 x **F** for the centre stitch, 3 x **H**, 1 x **AP** and 1 x **F** for the right-hand stitch and 3 x **H** and 1 x **F** for the left-hand stitch. Add three stitches between the raised stitches with **AI** and **AP**, angling them towards the centre of the flower. Tie down these three stitches to shape.

Small red bud

Work two stitches for each sepal using *raised effect – stitch length adjustment technique* for the inner stitch. Use **F** and

1–2 x **AM** at each end to taper for the right-hand sepal and **F** and 1–2 x **AP** at the tip to taper for the left-hand sepal. Stitch the bud using *vertical single layer technique with raised effect – general padding*. Use **AP** for the padding and work the centre stitch first with 3 x **H**, 1 x **BB** and 4 x **AP**. Add stitches on each side omitting **BB** and reducing the number of **H** and **AP** where necessary.

Berries

Work a horizontal padding stitch with 2 x **AW** at the centre of each berry. Work each berry with **AI**, **BE** and **AW** using *vertical single layer technique*. Tie down the outer stitches to shape.

LEAF GUIDE

Stems

___

NOTE: Where leaves overlap stems work the leaves first, otherwise work the stems first.

___

All main stems are stitched with **B** using *couching technique 1 – combination needle-koma method* and **AF** to taper where required.

Small stems are stitched with **AC** using aqua sewing thread and *couching technique 1 – combination needle-koma method* for stems with eight or more beads and *line of held thread – curved line method* for shorter lines.

Leaves

Refer to the guide on the facing page for colour and leaf placement.

Blue leaf cluster

Stems

Work stitches with **AQ** and tie down to shape. Stitch the leaves from foreground to background using *vertical single layer technique with raised effect*. Pad each leaf with a strategically placed vertical stitch using 2–3 x **AH**. Work each leaf with *vertical single layer technique* using **AS, S, BD** and **AV**. Tie down the outer stitches to shape.

Small leaves

The small leaves have no centre vein. Use the following bead and sewing thread combinations:

L1 – **AI** and **E**

L2 – **AI, R** and **AQ**

L3 – **AI** and **F** with sapphire blue thread

L4 – **AH** and **AS**

L5 – **AH** and **F** with sapphire blue thread

L6 – **AH, R** and **F** with sapphire blue thread

L7 – **AH** and **BC**

L8 – **AI** and **E** with sapphire blue thread

L9 – **AP** and **F** with sapphire blue thread

The leaves are stitched using *vertical single layer technique* (flat), *vertical single layer technique with raised effect* or *diagonal single layer*.

The raised effect on leaves with an **S** added in parentheses is created by using *raised effect – stitch length adjustment technique*. These leaves are worked in the same manner as the leaves for flower 4.

The raised effect on leaves with a **P** added in parentheses is created with *raised effect – general padding technique*.

a   P1 indicates padding with 2–3 vertical stitches along the centre using **AH** or **AV**.

b   P2 indicates leaves that have more than three stitches and are padded with 1–2 horizontal stitches, keeping a one bead space in from the edges.

Complete the leaves using *vertical single layer technique* and tie down the outer stitches to shape.

Leaves stitched with *diagonal single layer technique* are indicated with a **D** in parentheses. These leaves are worked in the same manner as the leaves for flower 4.

Large leaves

Use the following bead combinations:

LV1 – stitch the wide vein with **V, AI** and **I** using *diagonal single layer technique* in a left diagonal. Fill the remaining leaf area with **AH, AR** and **S** using *separated single layer technique*. Vary the combination and bead sequence in the stitches to create movement and form.

LV2 – work the leaf turnover at the tip with **I** using *diagonal single layer technique* in a left diagonal and beginning at the tip.

Stitch the centre vein with **D** using *couching technique 1 – combination needle-koma method*, adding **I** beads at each end to taper the line. Work the red dots on the right-hand side of the leaf using 1 x **H** for the small dot and 3 x **H** stitched in a Y pattern for the large dot.

Stitch the outer leaf section with **Y, BF** and **BA** using *separated single layer technique*, using **AU** to taper stitches where necessary.

Stitches for the left-hand side of the leaf extend from the outer edge to the leaf vein with **Y, BF** and/or **BA** as required for shading.

Work diagonal stitches on the right-hand side with **Y, BF** and/or **BA** up to positions in line with the red spots. Complete the right-hand side with **BF** and/or **BA** using closely spaced *scatter effect technique – singles*.

LV3 – work the leaf turnover at the tip with **AJ** and **AL** using *diagonal single layer technique* in a right diagonal and beginning at the tip with **AL**.

Stitch the wide vein in a similar manner to LV1 with **AI** and **AJ** using *diagonal single layer technique* in a right diagonal.

Stitch the outer leaf sections with **AM, BC, BA, L** and **AH** using *separated single layer technique*, using **AU** to taper stitches where necessary.

LV4 – Stitch the centre vein with **D** using *couching technique 1 – combination needle-koma method*, using **I** to taper each end.

Work each red dot with 3 x **H** stitched in a Y pattern. Stitch the outer leaf sections with **AC, AU** and **Y** using *separated single layer technique*, using **AC** and **AU** to taper stitches where necessary. Diagonal stitches on each side of the leaf are worked up to the positions in line with the red spots. Fill the inner leaf sections with **BA** and **BF** using *closely spaced scatter effect technique – singles*.

LV5 – Stitch the centre vein with **D** using *couching technique 1 – combination needle-koma method*, using **I** to taper each end. Fill the outer sections of the leaf with **AU** and **Y** using *separated single layer technique*. Use **AC** at the base of the leaf for shading. Work the inner section with **BA** using *scatter effect technique – singles*.

LV6 – There are three variations of this standard leaf, all stitched in the same manner using different colours and types of beads.

(1) – Use **AI** for the vein and **F** for the leaf.

(2) – Use **AI** for the vein and **E** for the leaf.

(3) – Use **I** for the vein and **S** and **AR** for the leaf.

LV7 – There are two variations of this leaf.

(1) – Stitch the leaf vein with **C** using *couching technique 1 – combination needle-koma method*, using **H** to taper each end. Where there is an attached stem, extend the vein line with **B** or **AF**.

Work the three stitches at the leaf tip with **AI**, **AQ** and **R** aligning the centre stitch with the vein. These stitches set the shape and movement of the leaf. Complete the leaf with diagonal stitches on each side with **R** and **AQ**. Tie down to shape.

(2) – Stitch the leaf in a similar manner to variation 1 adding **H** at the inner edge on the concave side.

LV8 – Work these leaves in a similar manner to LV6. Use **I** and **D** for the vein. Stitch the leaves with **K**, **BC** and **P** using random combinations and **AM** to taper stitches as necessary. **F** can also be added towards the base of the leaf or as the last bead abutting the vein line to create shading.

LV9 – There are two variations of this leaf.

(1) – Stitch the vein with **I**. Work the diagonal stitches on each side of the vein using *separated single layer technique*

with **AI**, placing 1 x **V** on the outer edge of each stitch. Complete the leaf with **AL**, **O** and **BA** using *separated single layer technique* and using **BA** as either the last or penultimate bead on each stitch.

(2) – Work in a similar manner to variation 1 omitting **BA**.

Background

Check to ensure that the overall size of 14cm x 26cm wide (5 ½" x 10 ¼") has been maintained and adjust if necessary. Beginning in the centre of the design and working outwards, fill the background with **AZ**, tapering with **AK** using *scatter effect technique – singles*. Re-check the sizing when ⅔ complete and adjust if necessary.

CONSTRUCTION

1 Complete the finishing process referring to page 132.

2 With the beading still on the frame, measure the beaded piece and check

that the size remains true. Using the pattern template, cut out the adhesive felt 2mm (¹⁄₁₆") smaller than the template. Peel away the backing and position the felt, adhesive side down over the wrong side of the embroidery and press gently. Check to ensure that the felt is positioned correctly. The stitching marking the outline should be visible outside the felt. Apply pressure to the felt in a sweeping motion from the centre outwards to ensure it is securely attached.

3 Remove the fabric from the frame and cut out leaving a 1cm (³⁄₈") seam allowance. At the rounded corners, work a line of small gathering stitches 6mm (¼") from the raw edge, beginning and ending 1.5cm (⁵⁄₈") from the corner. Pull up the gathers until the fabric hugs each corner.

Fold the seam allowance under on each side and press. Open out the seam allowance on each side. Apply a thin layer of craft glue to the edge of each seam allowance only. Fold in each seam allowance and glue in position, taking care to keep the glue clear of the seamline. The beads should sit slightly over the edge. Remove the stitched outline.

4   Mark the centre of the upper and lower long edges of the beaded fabric. Repeat on the zip of the folio frame and on the tape at the opposite edge of the folio.

Cut a 40cm (16") length of 12wt black *Wonderfil* sewing thread and thread into the no. 3 milliner's needle. Match the midpoints of the beaded fabric and the folio fabric tape. Beginning at the marked points and leaving half the thread hanging, work two small stitches to secure the thread. Stitch the fabric to the tape with ladder stitch, catching the fabric just under the beaded edge. Work to the corner and end off. Repeat for the second half.

Match the midpoints of the remaining long side of the beaded fabric and the zip tape. Using a 70cm (28") length of the same thread, secure the thread at the marked points, leaving half the thread hanging. Stitch the fabric to the zip tape, catching the fabric just under the beaded edge and 3mm (⅛") above the visible stitched line on the zip tape. Stitch to 1.5cm (⅝") past the rounded corner and leave the thread hanging. Return to the midpoint and stitch the second half, continuing along the side to finish at the corner. Using the left thread complete the stitching on the first half.

5   Gently steam the folio around the stitched seam, moulding it with fingers and leave to dry.

The list of equipment and tools required is not large and once collected, these will be all you need for your beading projects. Having the right tools and equipment will help make the process more efficient and more pleasurable.

FABRIC SELECTION AND TRANSFERRING DESIGNS TO FABRIC

Selecting a suitable fabric for the project is a prime consideration. The stretch, weight and weave of the fabric must support the design to ensure that the shape of the project and the desired aesthetics of the bead embroidery will be preserved even with frequent use.

Fabric that has a lot of stretch is not suitable for bead embroidery. Seed beads have a weight to them and can distort the weave of fabrics that have a lot of stretch. Suitable fabrics include quilting cotton, satin, polyester and silk with the qualities indicated. My personal preference is for either quilting cotton or silk depending on the project.

Print fabric

From time to time, we come across a patterned fabric where the design shouts out "BEAD ME". If the fabric is appropriate for bead embroidery and suitable for the project in mind, here is a ready design for embellishment. After that, it is only a matter of selecting the right beads, framing, deciding the techniques to use and beginning your bead embroidery.

Transferring designs to plain fabric

Transferring a design can be done in any of the following ways:

1 **Dressmaker's carbon paper:** This comes in different colours and it is a matter of choosing one that will show on the ground fabric. Transfer the design, placement guides and any required outlines onto tracing paper. Place the fabric on a smooth, hard surface and centre the tracing over the fabric, aligning the placement guides with the straight grain. Pin the tracing in place at each top corner. Slide the dressmaker's carbon, chalk side down, between the fabric and tracing. Using a stylus or spent ballpoint pen re-trace the design, pressing firmly. Ensure all lines have been transferred before removing the carbon and tracing.

TIP: It is useful to keep a spent ball point pen for this purpose.

2 **Ink jet printer:** To use a printer, first cut the fabric to paper size and stiffen by ironing freezer paper onto the back. Feed through the printer and peel off the freezer paper.

NOTE: This may take some practise and you will have to ensure that the printer can take the combined thickness of the fabric and freezer paper. It does result in neater design lines compared to the tracing method.

3 **Commercial printing:** This may not be a suitable option for one-off personal use and you will need to seek out someone who offers this service.

BEADING ON PRINTED FABRIC

FRAMES AND FRAMING UP

Any frame that supports a four-way stretch will be suitable. This includes stretcher bars, different variations of slate frames and traditional Japanese embroidery frames.

I would recommend that stretcher bars only be used for smaller projects as they are not conducive to making small adjustments to tension during the embroidery process should the need arise. Stretcher bars do not have the same ability to maintain tension as slate frames or the Japanese embroidery frame.

Preparing the fabric for framing

Check that the fabric size is suitable and fits the frame that you are going to use. If you are using a slate frame with tape attached to the bars, the fabric must be a good fit.

Determine which fabric direction has more stretch. In most fabrics, this lies along the weft, or across the fabric. In framing up, the side with the least stretch should be attached along the top and bottom bars of the frame, irrespective of design orientation.

If you are using a hybrid slate frame with no tape attached or a traditional Japanese embroidery frame, you will almost always need to sew on mounting fabric to make the base fabric a suitable size. The mounting fabric should be tightly woven cotton.

1   Reinforce the side edges of the fabric. Fold under a narrow hem on each side of the fabric along the warp direction and sew approximately 2mm ($^1/_{16}$") in from the folded edge along the warp of the fabric on either side.

2   Cut two pieces of mounting fabric of appropriate size. This fabric should be wider than the ground fabric (in the weft direction) by at least 5mm ($^3/_{16}$") on each side. It should extend the fabric length by 15cm (6") on each side for the hybrid slate frames or 30cm (12") for the traditional Japanese embroidery frame.

3   Machine stitch the mounting fabric to the ground fabric reinforcing the seams at the start and finish with double stitching approximately 1cm ($^3/_8$") back.

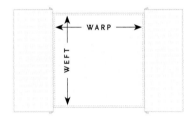

Traditional Japanese Frame

The traditional Japanese embroidery frame comprises the following components:

a) A pair of horizontal bars to be aligned to and to stretch the fabric in the warp direction.

b) A pair of weft bars to stretch the fabric in the weft direction

c) A pair of shuttle poles, each round and split in half lengthwise with nail holes at the end.

d) Two long shuttle nails for locking the shuttle pole in place when stretching the fabric in the warp direction.

e) Four weft pegs to lock the weft bars in position after stretching and tensioning the fabric in the weft direction.

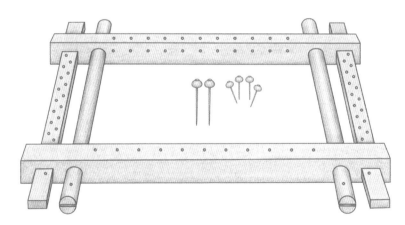

TRADITIONAL JAPANESE FRAME

FRAMING UP PROCESS

1 Insert the weft bars and one half of the shuttle pole on either side of the horizontal bars.

2 The warp of the fabric is framed up first. Drape the fabric across the frame, over the shuttle pole, lining up the warp of the fabric with the horizontal bars.

3 Insert the other half of the shuttle pole over the first half sandwiching the fabric. Leave some slack.

4 Insert the dowel nails with the point facing downward (diag 1).

5 Centre the fabric with some slack allowed and rotate the nail outwards from the centre in a one and three-quarters rotation. At the end of this, lock the nail in place with the weft bar.

6 Repeat for the remaining end. The fabric should be centred in the frame and taut on completion of step 6. If not, release the nails and make adjustments to steps 5 and 6 until the correct tension is achieved.

7 Push the horizontal bars until they abut the edge of the fabric (diag 2).

8 Lace the fabric to the horizontal bars, starting from the right and working towards the left.

9 Tie the lacing thread to the first hole of the horizontal bar and ensure it is secure.

10 Bring the needle down through the hole and come up in the fabric, just inside the seam allowance, a quarter of the distance between the last and next holes.

11 Bring the needle down through the fabric at the three-quarter distance between the last and next holes.

12 Bring the needle up between the fabric and the horizontal bar and

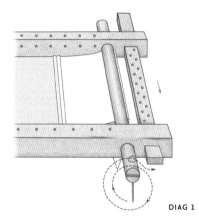

DIAG 1

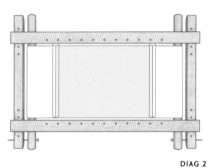

DIAG 2

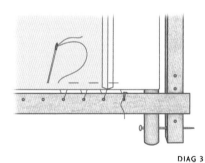

DIAG 3

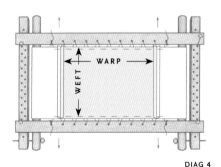

DIAG 4

TRADITIONAL JAPANESE FRAME
FRAMING UP PROCESS

repeat steps 10 and 11 until the end is reached finishing with step 11 (diag 3).

13 Using an awl and starting from the beginning of the thread at the right-hand side, pull the lacing thread firmly. Continue for each section to remove excess thread. When the end is reached, secure the thread by looping it through the frame twice and tie off.

14 Repeat steps 9 to 13 for the remaining side.

15 Insert the weft pegs in the holes on the weft bars, on the inner side of the horizontal bars. To increase tension, pull the horizontal bars further apart and reinsert the pegs to hold the desired tension (diag 4).

Slate Frames

There are different variations of slate frames available but they all consist of the following parts:

(a) a pair of horizontal bars with holes on each end and (b) a pair of side bars with multiple holes on each end to allow for adjustments for different fabric sizes.

FRAMING UP PROCESS

Fold under 6mm (¼") along the warp and press. Sew a 4mm (5/32") seam along this folded edge. If required, sew end cloths along the weft to extend the length of the fabric.

1 If the slate frame has a tape attached to the horizontal bars, centre the fabric and attach it to the tape with back stitches with a seam allowance of approximately 5mm (3/16"). Sew out from the centre to one side and then the other. Do likewise for the other end with the second horizontal bar.

2 If the horizontal bars have no tape attached, secure the fabric to the bar

as per instructions for the frame. I use a hybrid slate frame that is based on the design of the traditional Chinese embroidery frame. It has no tape attached to it. Instead it has a groove into which the fabric extension pieces are secured and held in place with a wedge strip (diag 5).

The cotton fabric is then rolled around the horizontal bars until the design is centred. The cotton fabric should wrap around the horizontal bars at least twice (diag 6).

3 Position the weft bars into the slots of the horizontal bars. Insert the pins and adjust for tension by placing them into the appropriate holes (diag 7).

This step applies to both types of slate frame.

4 Turn the frame so that the side bar is positioned in a left-right direction to you. Secure the lacing thread to the horizontal bar on the right-hand side and turn the thread inwards around the end of the bar to secure it.

5 Bring the needle and thread under the side bar and up through the fabric approximately 1cm (³/₈") in from the edge. This first stitch should abut the horizontal bar.

6 Re-enter the fabric approximately 2cm (³/₄") along to the left and 1cm (³/₈") in from the edge.

7 Bring the needle up through the fabric approximately 1cm (³/₈") along to the left from the last stitch and just inside the hem line.

8 Loop the needle and thread over the

side bar. Bring the needle up through the fabric 1cm (³/₈") in from the edge and approximately 5mm (³/₁₆") along to the left of the last stitch. Repeat steps 6 to 8 until the end (diags 8–9).

Finish with step 7.

9 Do likewise for the remaining side with steps 4 to 8.

10 Adjust by pulling and tightening the lacing thread to achieve the desired tension. Secure the lacing thread by wrapping it around the frame (diag 10).

NOTE: *The lacing thread used should be sufficiently strong. Cotton thread such as DMC broder spécial size 16 or Presencia Algodon Tri-Finca size 6 or 6½ are suitable.*

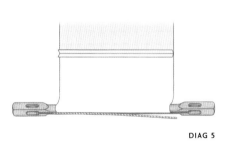

DIAG 5

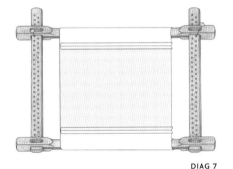

DIAG 7

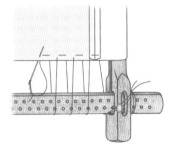

DIAG 9

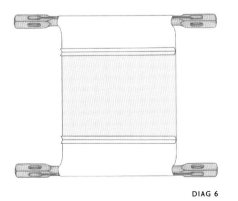

DIAG 6

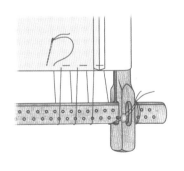

DIAG 8

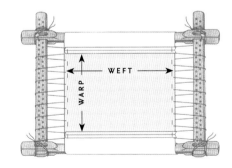

DIAG 10

SLATE FRAME FRAMING UP PROCESS

THREADS

Cotton or silk threads can be used. As a general rule, cotton threads in either black or white in a 50 weight are used. I favour a lighter 60 thread weight that I have found to be ideal for almost all design situations. This thread is not as commonly available.

Polycotton threads may also be used but should be tested to ensure compatibility with the design and that lines of beads lie as they should.

White thread is nearly always used for the design embroidery and black thread is used for stitching the background if black or very dark coloured beads are used. Variations from this will be design driven.

In certain design situations coloured cotton threads or stranded embroidery floss may be used. When used with transparent beads they add a subtle colour and provide delicate colour contrast.

Synthetic beading threads, although stronger, are not suitable as they do not always sit well on the fabric surface so I tend to avoid them.

Threads should not be waxed or treated with thread conditioners prior to embroidery as this will negatively impact the finishing process.

NEEDLES

Bead Embroidery:

The needles used should provide the practitioner with good control and be fine enough to slip through small beads without difficulty. Normal beading needles are too soft for the precise control required for Japanese-style bead embroidery.

Needles that have been tested and found suitable include:

John James Gold and Glide no.11

Clover Black Gold no.9

Clover quilting betweens no.11 and 12.

My personal favourite and preferred needles are:

Japanese embroidery M2 (for beading) and M3 (for couching) These may be more difficult to obtain as they are specialised needles.

Roxanne sharp no.12 (for beading) and sharp no.10 (for couching)

Other applications:

Needles are also required for lacing up the fabric. No.'s 1 to 3 milliner's needles or a no. 3 long darner are suitable for this job. These needles are long and easier to manoeuvre for the lacing process.

To provide contrast and definition, overlapping petals were worked alternately with white and red coloured threads.

TEKOBARI OR LAYING TOOL

The tekobari is a laying tool used in traditional silk embroidery to spread, tension and lay the silk threads. This same tool is used in bead embroidery where it is used to tension and guide the threads as stitches are made. It is also used to help change the direction of beads or untwist a thread as required. In place of a tekobari, a laying tool or equivalent with a tapered point can be used.

KOMA

Koma are wooden bobbins with squared edges. They are used to help maintain tension and to position the beads that are being couched. Because of the squared edges, they will not roll on the fabric. The koma are used as a pair secured together with a rubber band or some other suitable binding. The pair sits snugly and comfortably in the palm of the hand and allows movement of the fingers. In this way, the thread can be tensioned and the fingers can assist in manipulating the beads at the same time while couching progresses.

Always ensure that the thread sits under the koma while couching as this brings the beads nearer to the fabric surface.

SCISSORS
Embroidery Scissors

For practitioners of Japanese embroidery, Japanese-made flat shear scissors that have sharp tips are used. Scissors can be very personal, so select a pair that you are comfortable with. They must be small, with a sharp, fine tip to allow precise cutting close to the fabric.

A pair of scissors for metal threads is a useful addition to the list of equipment.

Metal threads work well with beads and can be incorporated into the bead embroidery.

Fabric Scissors

It is handy to have a pair of sharp fabric scissors on hand for cutting fabric. There is no specific recommendation for these and personal preference should be your guide.

Paper Scissors

A pair of scissors is also required for cutting out paper templates. It is always wise to keep separate paper and fabric scissors as cutting paper may blunt the edge of a good pair of scissors.

BEAD SHOE

A bead shoe is traditionally made from a piece of felt approximately 10cm (4") square. As the needle tends to catch on the felt, beading mat material is a very good alternative.

Mitre the two top corners of the square by squeezing between thumb and index finger of both hands. Bring the two mitred corners to meet at the midpoint of the top edge of the square. A bead shoe in the form of a 'shovel' is created. Stitch in place with overcast stitch to maintain the shape. These are used to contain the beads during the embroidery process and allow the beads to be brought close to the area being worked. Make up and use several bead shoes at any time. When picking up beads with the needle use a scooping motion.

G-CLAMPS

It is usual practice to work with both hands in a coordinated manner, with the right hand on top and the left hand below the frame. G-clamps enable the frame to be held firmly to the table leaving the hands free. If a traditional embroidery frame or larger slate frame is used, the frame is first positioned between two flat surfaces such as two tables or on top of a pair of trestles and then clamped in position to prevent movement.

BEAD SCOOP

There are different models of bead scoops available. An elongated and tapered shape is preferable for bead embroidery.

PAIR OF SMALL PLIERS

These are optional but are useful for breaking beads should an odd shaped one be found. This avoids the need to remove and restring beads. An awl can also be used for this purpose but pliers are more user-friendly.

DRESSMAKING PINS

These are used for holding down the paper template or as a temporary marker when making measurements. There are different types of dressmaking pins available and glass-head pins are preferred.

DRAWING EQUIPMENT

This is optional but there may be times when you wish to re-mark a design line or make changes. I recommend a size 0.3 HB mechanical pencil or an acid-free size 0.1 pigment pen, available in different colours.

TAPE MEASURE AND RULER

For those times when you need to measure fabric, check for accurate measurements or draw in guidelines, it is useful to have these handy.

TWEEZERS

These are again optional and may be useful for removing stitches. Tweezers with a pointed tip are preferred and nothing beats a pair of *Gingher* tweezers.

DRESSMAKER'S CARBON PAPER

For tracing designs to fabric, this comes in different colours and is available in multi-colour packs. The *Clover Chacopy* carbon paper is recommended. This is available in 5-sheet packs in 5 colours.

GILDING PENS

Occasionally, the design can be enhanced by adding some gilding so it is useful to have one of these.

Liquid gilt applied with a small paint brush is also appropriate.

In this section common practices that apply to Japanese-style bead embroidery are introduced. These are practices that should, in time, become automatic and be applied without even thinking.

THE BEADS

Beads, like threads, can have slight colour variations between production batches. If this is a cause for concern in a design, ensure you have sufficient beads to complete the project.

Japanese beads are fairly consistent in size. From time to time, there will be a bead that is smaller than usual. Do not discard these—they are gold! Situations will arise, especially at the end of a line or in tight corners, where a full-size bead will not fit and this is the time to use them.

If you are working on a symmetrical project, divide the beads into two before commencing.

THE PIN STITCH

A pin stitch is a small stitch the size of a needle point. When properly executed this stitch cannot be felt on the face of the fabric.

Pin stitch is used every time a thread is started and ended off. To start, make a knot in the thread. Bring the needle to the front and make two pin stitches in a back stitch motion or perpendicular to each other. Ensure that these pin stitches are made in an area that will be covered by the bead embroidery. To finish off, make three pin stitches, again under a bead-embroidered area. These stitches should be done as back stitches or in

perpendicular positions to one another to secure the last stitch. Bring the thread to the front after the last stitch and cut close to the surface.

The pin stitch also has an important role in the embroidery process. It is used to ensure that a stitch is secured in position before moving on to the next stitch. This removes any likelihood of the stitch line moving and helps maintain the integrity of the stitches.

Pin stitch after each line of beads. The pin stitch lies along the direction of the stitch line except for any raised effect, in which case, the pin stitch will be made back under the stitch.

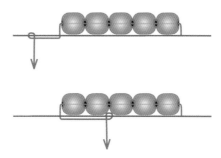

CARRYING THREADS

Threads may be carried but not more than 1cm (3/8"). For any greater distance, pin stitches at intervals of no more than 1cm (3/8") must be made. If the distance is more than 3cm (1¼"), it is recommended that consideration be given to finishing the thread and restarting.

THREAD THICKNESS

A double thread is used for any stitch involved in going through a bead. For couching or tying down a stitch, a single thread can be used. The double thread is achieved by threading a single thread through the needle and knotting both ends together.

SPACING FOR COUCHING

When securing a length of beads, couching will be at intervals of every bead or every two beads. Where a firmer line is required or the curve of a line is tighter, couch at every bead interval, otherwise, intervals of two beads are adequate. The first and last couching stitch must always be one bead away from the end.

PATTERN OUTLINE

The transfer of a pattern outline to the fabric is done with *Japanese running stitch* for curved lines or *line of held thread technique* for straight lines.

Japanese running stitch

1   Bring the needle to the front and make a stitch along the line approximately 5mm–9mm (3/16"–3/8"). The length of the stitch will depend on the curve. The tighter the curve the shorter the stitch.

2   Bring the needle to the front a pin stitch away from the end of the last stitch and repeat the two steps.

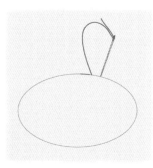

3   For best results work Japanese running stitch in a clockwise direction.

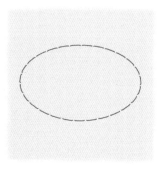

Line of held thread technique

1   Bring the needle to the front at one end of the line and take it to the back at the other end. This creates a plumb line, true and straight.

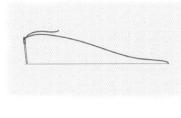

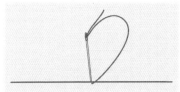

2   Tie down the stitch. The first stitch is made at the midpoint of the thread line.

3   Continue to tie down the thread at midpoints between the divided sections of the thread. Continue until the thread is fully tied along the line and the stitching interval is no less than 1cm (3/8"). Dividing and tying down the thread sequentially at the midpoints of sections ensures that the thread is secured along the line with the greatest accuracy.

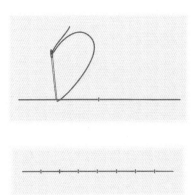

If using a paper template for the project, pin in position on the fabric or secure with tacking stitches. The pins should be placed in an outward direction, with at least one pin in each corner of the design. For larger outlines the tacking method should be used for greater accuracy.

Where there are corners or points in the outline extend the two corner stitches approximately 5mm (3/16") beyond the points so that they cross each other. This will give an accurate reading to the exact position of the corner or point.

Where an outline is made up of two sides from the same template, make a mark to indicate the position the template is facing. When marking the template for the remaining side use the same template but flip it over so that you are using the mirror image.

If a line of beads is stitched around the design, work it outside the outlining thread. The outlining thread is taken out after the beading is complete but before assembly. It is therefore useful to use a contrasting colour thread from the ground fabric to make this easier.

MAINTAINING CORRECT SIZING

If accurate sizing is a concern, e.g. the piece is sized to fit a specific box top, conduct regular checks during the embroidery process. Everyone stitches differently and different stitch tension can result in minor changes in sizing. The embroidery should be one bead width outside the pattern template. If this is not the case, adjustments need to be made accordingly and it is better and easier to do it during the embroidery process than when the whole piece is complete.

Techniques for Japanese-style bead embroidery are not complicated. All stitches are laid stitches according to the technique requirement and each of these techniques creates a visual movement. When the techniques are applied to a design, together they create a harmonious visual movement and perspective. This is augmented by the correct selection of beads, size, shape and colour, which add texture and further accentuate dimensional perspective.

Some concepts to bear in mind:

Bead size: Using different size beads in the same stitch will visually taper a line.

Colour: Colour changes within the same line of beads will also visually taper a line. A deeper colour is applied for this purpose. Changes in bead size and colour can be used concurrently to further enhance tapering.

Spacing: Increasing the space between beads at the end of a line will further enhance the tapering effect.

Negative space: When appropriately used can result in creating visual interest. It is a design concept that is all too frequently forgotten.

The one-point space: In Japanese embroidery, the one-point space is left between overlapping motifs to create dimensional perspective. This can also be used judiciously in bead embroidery for the same purpose. Leaving a gap between motifs will create the same dimensional perspective. The gap usually ranges from 0.5–1 size 15 bead space.

Density: In this respect, there should be a balance between solidly filled and lightly filled areas within the design.

Less is more: This cannot be emphasised enough. Each bead needs its own space to shine and show off its beauty. Overcrowding will not only prevent this, it will also push the beads out of their correct position and distort the lines and flow of the design.

'Feel' your design: In the process of bead embroidery let your intuition also be your guide. This is especially the case when stitching florals. When stitches are lined up too perfectly, they can look artificial and stiff. Cultivate a 'feel' for your stitches so that they flow with the overall design.

ONE POINT SPACE SEPARATING FLOWER SECTIONS

DENSITY

On completion of the bead embroidery, every piece goes through a finishing process before assembly to tidy up loose ends and, more importantly, settle the beads and set the embroidery.

1 Do a final size check of the embroidery and check that the tension is still correct. Re-tension if necessary.

2 Check the back of the embroidery and ensure there are no stray loops or threads. If there are you need to do one of the following:

a) If the loops are short, thread up a separate needle and anchor this with two pin stitches at a distance 5mm (3/16") longer than the loop. Hook the loop with the thread and needle and pull until it lays flat against the fabric. Finish with three pin stitches and make sure these are hidden behind beads.

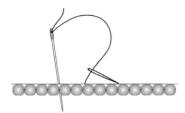

b) If the loops are long and there is sufficient length to thread through a needle, do so and secure the thread with three pin stitches behind adjacent beads.

3 With the completed embroidery still on the frame, spray with water from the back and rub on the wrong side to ensure that the water has fully penetrated all threads.

4 Place the frame with the wrong side uppermost on a sunny window sill to dry. Alternatively, place near a heater—always with the wrong side to the heat. This gentle heat and the dampening help to settle and set the fabric and threads.

5 When the piece is dry, it can be removed from the frame and constructed into the planned project.

THE
TECHNIQUES OF
JAPANESE-STYLE
BEAD EMBROIDERY

There are three foundation principles that apply to every stitch made that will guarantee a superior outcome. These principles apply whether it is a single bead stitch, a line of beads, a couching stitch and even the pin stitch. If applied incorrectly, the design may be distorted by the stitch being out of position and/or out of line in relation to other stitches. These three fundamentals, when applied correctly, ensure a harmony and fluidity of movement to the embroidery.

Stitch Direction

The direction determines the way a stitch is pulled, which in turn determines how that stitch will sit in relation to surrounding stitches.

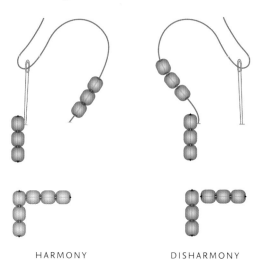

HARMONY   DISHARMONY

Stitch Placement

This refers to the position where the needle comes up and goes down through the fabric. This determines the stitch line, which in turn creates the visual movement of the design

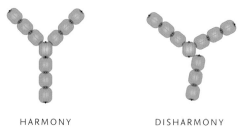

HARMONY   DISHARMONY

Stitch Length

The length of each stitch must be appropriate for the number of beads. If the stitch is too short, the beads will not lie smooth and flat. If it is too long, the beads will wobble with the extra space and distort the stitch lines.

TOO SHORT   TOO LONG   CORRECT

SINGLE STITCHES

The simplest stitch in bead embroidery is that of a single stitch loaded with one or more beads. This stitch can be applied in different ways and combinations to create different effects, e.g. a simple flower is achieved by stitching carefully placed single stitches.

Stitches within each technique introduced are applied in a specific and prescribed method to achieve an overall effect. For each single stitch the key is to maintain correct stitch direction, stitch placement and stitch length.

single stitch one bead

single stitch multiple bead

Line of Staggered Diagonals

This technique creates a line with a sequence of diagonal stitches of two or three beads for each stitch. These diagonal stitches introduce movement within the line and give emphasis to the curve.

To emphasise a line that curves in a clockwise direction, stitching will proceed so that the clockwise movement is maintained. Stitches are oriented in an upper right to lower left direction **relative to the contour of the curve.** This technique can be worked as a 3-step or 4-step method, with the 4-step method creating a thicker line.

3-step method (clockwise)

Begin with a single stitch of one bead that lies parallel to the curve and follow with stitches of two beads oriented in an upper right to lower left direction. Each stitch begins approximately halfway along the previous stitch.

Bring the needle up at around the midpoint of the previous stitch and make a second diagonal stitch. Some slight adjustments will be made to this position depending on the arc of the curve. Repeat this step until the end, finishing with a single bead stitch for a tapered ending. Remember to make a pin stitch after each stitch in the direction of the bead.
It will help the beads to sit flat.

Beginning and ending with a single bead creates a tapered effect. If tapering is not required, omit the stitch with a single bead and begin with a stitch of two beads.

4-step method (clockwise)

Begin with a single stitch of one bead that lies parallel to the curve and follow with a second and third stitch of two and three beads respectively in an upper right to lower left direction **relative to the contour of the curve**. These second and third stitches begin approximately two-thirds up the previous stitch. Thereafter, stitches of three beads are made, all beginning approximately two-thirds up the previous stitches. Repeat this step until the end. If a tapered end is required, reduce the number of beads for the last two stitches to two beads and then one bead. Again, if tapering is not required, omit the first and last two stitches of one and two beads.

Remember to make a pin stitch after each stitch in the direction of the bead. It will help the beads sit flat.

If a slightly raised effect is desired, make the pin stitch back under the stitch itself. This should be applied only to stitches with three beads as it will not work for one or two bead stitches.

Counter-clockwise lines

At times the design line portrays a counter-clockwise movement. In this case, stitching progresses in the same manner as the clockwise curves except the stitches lie in an upper left to lower right diagonal direction **relative to the contour of the curve.**

LINE OF HELD THREAD

In Japanese embroidery, this technique is used to create linear effects by holding long stitches in place along a line, often curved, with spaced stitches holding them in place. These stitches are referred to as tie-down stitches to distinguish them from couching stitches that are used in relation to couching techniques.

In bead embroidery this technique is used to hold a line of beads along a design line. It is suitable for relatively shorter lines and it is recommended that the stitch lengths using this technique do not exceed 2cm (3/4") in length. A good estimation of stitch length, which should take into account the space that will be taken up by the tie-down stitches, is necessary. For a ten-bead length, a good thread allowance is about the length of one and a half beads.

Line of held thread— Straight line

1   Bring the needle to the front at one end of the line, pick up the required number of beads and re-enter the fabric at the other end. Remember to take into account the thread allowance.

2   Using the same needle and thread, tie down the stitch starting from one end. The first stitch is one bead in from the edge and thereafter is a two bead interval. The last stitch will be one bead before the end, even if it is out of line with the two bead interval.

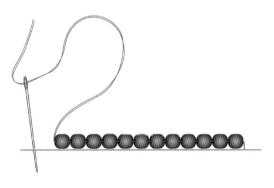

Line of held thread— Curved Line

1   Bring the needle to the front at one end of the line, pick up the required number of beads and re-enter the fabric at the other end. Remember to take into account the thread allowance.

2   Using the same needle and thread, make the first tie-down stitch at the midpoint of the length of beads.

3   Work the first half of the divided line. The next stitch will tie down the thread at the midpoint between the stitch from step 2 and the end of the design line. Continue in a similar manner, each time tying down the thread to the design line at the midpoints of new sections created until the tie-down stitches are two beads apart.

4   Work the second half in the same manner

Note: If the curve of the design line is tight, the interval of tie-down stitches may need to be every bead to secure a smooth curve.

Line of Held Thread—Circle

This method is used to create a circle of beads, usually encircling a bead or shape.

1 Bring the needle to the front at a point along the line of the circle.

2 Pick up the number of beads required to create the circle. Take the needle through the first one or two beads and re-enter the fabric along the stitch line. For small circles one bead is appropriate but for larger circles, two will provide better control. Bring the needle to the front further along the circle. Park the needle in the fabric.

3 With a second needle and single strand, tie-down between the beads beginning at the point opposite the first bead and then at midpoints between these positions. Continue tying down between each bead, shaping the circle with the tie-down stitches as necessary.

4 On completion, pick up the parked needle and give it a gentle pull to tension the circle of beads. Make a pin stitch to secure and continue the beading process.

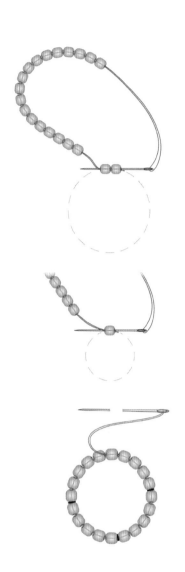

COUCHED LINES

Couching differs from the **line of held thread method** in that the line of beads is couched sequentially from the end with a separate needle. The needle with the line of beads is taken through the fabric only after all the couching stitches are complete. Couching is the preferred method when the lines are long or when the area to be filled is large.

General couching principles

The couching technique is worked with the aid of koma to achieve tension and help with positioning the beads to the next couching point. The mantra for couching is *'stitch... tension... position... stitch... tension... etc.'* After every stitch, tension must be retained with a soft pull on the koma. Follow this by moving the koma and positioning the beads to the next couching stitch. The extra tensioning will settle the beads into position especially around curves.

Transferring beads to the koma

Before commencing, the koma need to be prepared and the beads transferred onto a double thread, which will be wound around the koma.

1 The koma are used as a pair secured with a rubber band or some other suitable binding such as a length of 1cm (3/8") twill tape.

   Take an appropriate length of thread, double it over and make a knot at the end. If you are working with loose beads, it will need to be threaded through a needle at this point before doubling and attaching to the pair of komas. As a guide, for every metre length of beads, add between 50cm–80cm (20"–32") extra to the doubled length of thread. This will provide an allowance to accommodate finishing and the couching stitches. 3m (3yd 10") is the maximum length as anything longer will be difficult to handle.

2 Tie the knotted end to the koma and wind the thread around the pair.

3 **Transferring beads to the threads on the koma**

   If the beads come in hanks: Japanese beads are in a standard 1m (40") length for each hank. Attach your doubled thread to that of the hank thread and push the beads over to the doubled thread.

   If the beads are loose: pour a good amount into a bead shoe and pick up in a quick scooping motion with the needle from the koma. Each scoop will generally pick up several beads and the thread will be loaded up in no time. Another way is to load the beads with the aid of a bead spinner. The use of a bead spinner is purely optional.

Starting and ending the couching process

The following steps are standard for all couched techniques.

1 If there is no needle attached to the koma, thread the doubled thread through a needle. For this purpose a larger needle such as a no. 9 sharp will be suitable. The eye of a beading needle is too small to thread a doubled thread through.

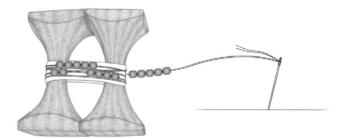

2 Bring the needle down through the fabric at the point where the first couched bead will sit. Make three pin stitches as if you were finishing the stitch, bring the needle to the front and cut off the end of the thread.

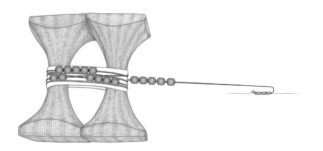

3 Thread the couching needle with a single strand. Knot the thread and make the two usual starting pin stitches and commence couching.

4 Start couching at the first bead and then every two beads

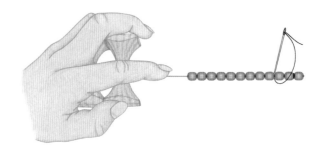

5 To end, cut the thread approximately 6cm (2 ⅜") from the last bead. Thread up and take the needle down through the fabric at the end of the line. Give a little tug to re-tension before finishing with three pin stitches. Finish off the couching thread similarly with three pin stitches. The last couching stitch is one bead from the end.

Couching Technique 1

Combination Needle-Koma Method

This technique is not a true couching technique in the pure sense but is a hybrid using the principles drawn from **couching** and **line of held thread** techniques. It is best done so that the working order proceeds in a **clockwise direction** and is suitable for stitching lines that are too long for the **line of held thread** to be effective yet not long enough for the true couching method to be applied.

1 After the usual pin stitches, bring the needle up at the starting point and pick up the estimated number of beads required for the line.

2 Wind the needle and excess thread onto the koma.

3 Starting from the first bead, couch sequentially at two bead intervals along the line. Remember the couching mantra.

4 Tension after each couching stitch by pulling on the koma.

5 With the help of the koma and keeping the thread under tension, position the beads to the next couching position and make the next couching stitch.

6 Repeat steps 4 and 5 to the end of the line finishing with the last couching stitch one bead from the end.

7 Unwind the thread from the koma, remove any excess beads and go down through the fabric at the end of the design line. Give a final tensioning tug and make a pin stitch to secure the line. The pin stitch is placed along the direction of the design line.

8 The needle and thread can travel to the next section to be stitched.

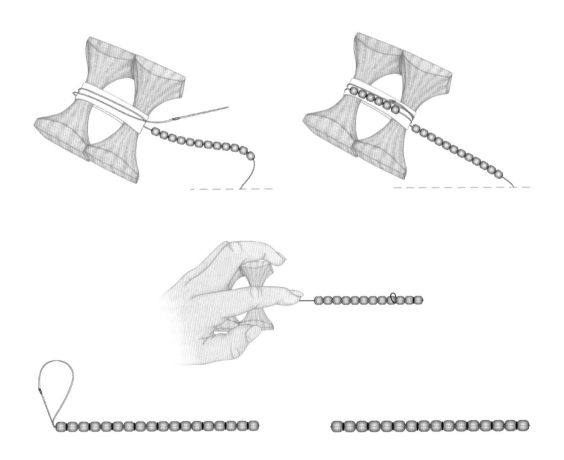

Couching Technique 3

To and Fro

In this technique lines of beads are couched beginning along one outside edge of the motif. When the end is reached, the line turns and is couched back in the opposite direction. This process is repeated until the whole motif is covered.

This produces a visually continuous flow of uninterrupted lines. It is useful for filling regularly shaped areas. Used judiciously, it can also be employed as a means to create a regularly shaped area within another area.

Turning the corners at each end is an area that requires attention as the lines must lie true.

1   Start the couching process.

2   Approximately 7mm (5/16") from the end, make a pin stitch with the couching thread and bring the couching needle and thread to the front at the turning point. Measure out the number of beads required to complete the line and couch the koma thread.

3   The thread should be couched one point back from the perceived turning point to allow for the slight pull back when the thread is turned. Make a pin stitch with the couching thread to secure this corner stitch.

4   Go back to the line of beads and couch between each one for the last 7mm (5/16") that were left in step 2. This step ensures that the line will remain true especially at the turning edge.

5   Turn the koma thread and couch it right against the edge in a position that will start the next line of beads parallel to the first. This point will be half a bead width from the edge of the previous line of beads. Make a pin stitch to secure the couching stitch. The couching stitch that turns the

koma thread should be made in the direction against the turn of the koma thread for a firm hold. When properly done, all the turning and pin stitches will not be visible.

6   Continue couching back along the line, offsetting the couching stitch for every two beads with the couching stitches of the first line.

7   Repeat steps 2–6 until the area is complete.

8   End the couching process.

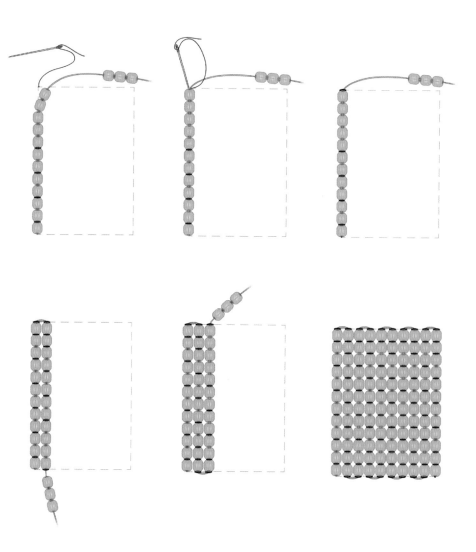

Couching Technique 4

Round and Round

This technique produces a continuous line of couching following the shape of the motif until it is solidly filled. The shape is maintained and the line movement follows around the shape. This technique will help maintain and emphasise the motif within the design.

Couching begins with the outline of the motif in a clockwise direction and continues inwards until the motif is solidly filled. The couching of each line is offset against that of the adjoining line.

For this technique, where corners exist in the motif design, turning these is slightly different to that for **Couching Technique 3**.

Start the couching process at a corner and couch following the shape until the next corner is reached.

Corners can be worked in one of two ways:

If the line of beads currently being couched is to form the corner stitch:

1 About 7mm (5/16") from the end stop the couching and measure and put in place the appropriate number of beads to complete the line to the corner. Make the last couching stitch for the line to secure it in place. This stitch should be as small as possible. Make a pin stitch after this stitch to secure.

2 Turn the koma thread and couch right up against the edge of the last bead in a position that will begin the next line and, at the same time, form a sharp corner with the first line of beads. Pin stitch to secure this stitch.

3 Return and couch the last few beads of the first line, spacing the beads as appropriate. Pin stitch on completion.

4 Couch the first bead of the second line and proceed with normal couching principles.

5 When the motif is solidly filled, end the couching process

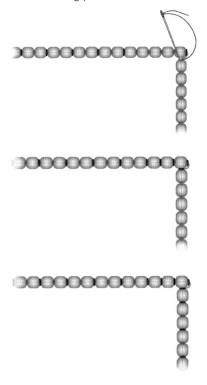

If the line currently being couched does not form the corner stitch, and the corner stitch is to be created by the second line of beads:

The last bead will stop a bead space before the corner. As with the previous method, about 7mm (5/16") from the last bead, stop couching, measure and put in place the appropriate number of beads to complete the line. Make the last couching stitch for the line. This stitch should be as small as possible. Make a pin stitch to secure this.

1 Turn the koma thread and couch it in a position that will start the next line of beads.

2 Again, check that the first bead of this line is in the right position to form a sharp corner with the beads of the first line. Pin stitch to secure this stitch.

3 Return and couch the last few beads of the first line, spacing the beads as appropriate. Pin stitch on completion.

4 Couch the first bead of the second line and proceed with normal couching principles.

5 When the motif is solidly filled, end the couching process

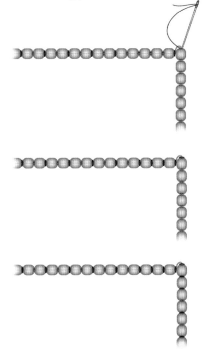

Where a corner in the motif is very sharp, it may not be possible to fill the space right at the very tip with the beads in use. In these instances, leave the space and continue to complete the overall couching. These spaces are left and filled individually with a smaller size bead.

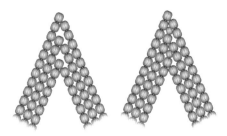

The single layer techniques are used to fill a motif from edge to edge. There are several techniques within this category and each creates a different movement and visual impression.

HORIZONTAL LAYER

- The stitches are oriented horizontally to the motif.

- Stitches are parallel to each other.

- Commence the first stitch in a spot with a good line of reference. Work parallel stitches aligned to this stitch to complete.

- Consider using smaller beads to assist with rounded edges at both ends of the motif.

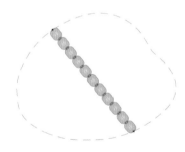

VERTICAL LAYER

Vertical layer stitches are oriented in the vertical direction of a design motif. They are more often than not used to stitch flower petals as the lines on completion simulate the opening of a flower.

- Stitch the first line of beads down the centre of the motif dividing it in half.

- One half is completed first and then the other. There are exceptions to this and these circumstances will be design driven.

- The stitches are either parallel or slightly tapered towards the base of the motif.

- Smaller beads will again assist in achieving rounded edges or tapering when applied appropriately.

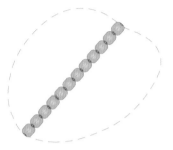

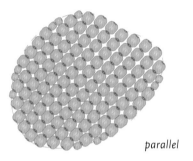

parallel

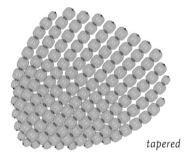

tapered

DIAGONAL LAYER

Of all the techniques, this gives the most movement to a motif from a design point of view.

- The diagonal stitches can be right or left diagonals.

- Right diagonals lie in an upper right to lower left direction **in relation to the axis of the motif being stitched**, while the left diagonals lie in an upper left to lower right direction.

- When stitching this technique, attention must be paid to the curve

and the angle of the diagonal stitches are adjusted accordingly to present a fluid and harmonious movement. Generally, the angle of the diagonal stitches should be relatively steep, between 50–60 degrees, as a flatter diagonal stitch will give less movement.

- Right diagonals should be stitched in a clockwise progression and left diagonals in a counter-clockwise progression for best results.

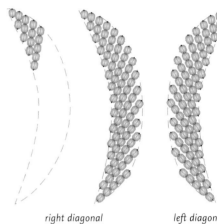

right diagonal   *left diagonal*

SEPARATED SINGLE LAYER

This technique is appropriate for any design motif that has a mid-line separating the left and right sides, e.g. leaves, feathers. It is based on the *diagonal layer technique*. The right side of the two sections is stitched with right diagonal stitches and the left side with left diagonal stitches.

- The rules that apply to the *diagonal layer technique* also apply here.

- When stitching with this technique, the larger side of the motif, therefore being the more prominent side, is stitched first. Once completed, it provides a good visual to help ascertain the angle of the stitches for the second side to create a harmonious balance of the two sides.

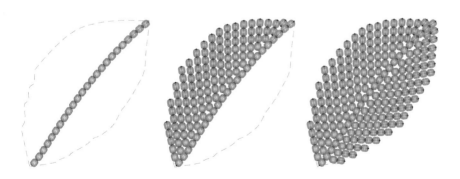

RAISED EFFECT

To give added dimension to the embroidery raised effects can be introduced. This is achieved with either one of the following:

Adjusting stitch length

This is generally used for smaller motifs, areas and shorter lines

- In this method, one, two or three additional beads are added to the stitch causing it to rise up from the fabric surface.

- There are always stitches on either side abutting the raised stitch to give it support.

- Use of colour and changes in bead sizes will help emphasise and enhance the raised effect.

- This technique can be applied with any of the *single layer techniques* and *long and short techniques* to create greater movement, texture and dimensional perspective.

143

Padding

This technique gives a greater raised effect with more stability. It is suitable for larger motifs with longer stitch lengths. Different effects can be created by the correct placement of padding. Beads are used for the padding.

There are two ways to apply padding:

Outline only padding

This method of padding, which is only applied along the outline of a motif, results in a prominent line on the outer edge. The padding line is approximately one size 15 bead space in from the design lines.

General padding

General padding creates a raised effect for the entire motif, not just the outline. When applying general padding, the following principles apply:

- Padding is always in the opposite direction to the ultimate surface embroidery.
- **Line of held thread technique** is used to apply padding.
- Padding lines begin and end one size 15 bead space in from the design line.
- A tapering effect can be achieved by increasing the space between padding lines and dropping the last two stitches.

When applying surface stitching to padded areas, always stitch from the outer edge in. Surface stitching can also incorporate more than a single technique, particularly if the motif is large, to achieve the desired effect.

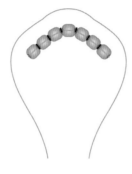 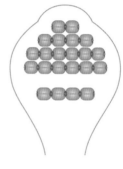 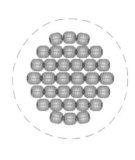

outline only   *tapered*   *general*

LONG AND SHORT STITCHES

This technique is suitable to cover larger areas and where dimensional perspective is desired.

It is often used for shapes that converge such as flower petals.

1 Determine the desired shape and its flow lines.

2 Identify the centre and begin the first stitch line at this point.

3 Work one side first with long and short stitches following the flow lines identified in step 1. When the first side is complete, work the second side in a similar manner.

NOTE: Padding may be added to create greater dimension. This is often in the form of outline only padding.

---

4 Add second and third rows as necessary, with long and short lines of beads, following the flow lines. Change the colour of beads to shade as desired.

5 As work progresses towards the centre and space diminishes, smaller beads can be used. Do not space beads too closely. Allow to fade out towards the centre.

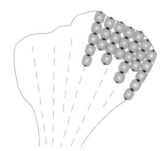 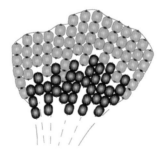 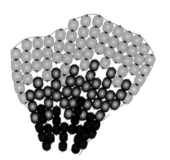

In this technique, the surface of a completed project or design is completely covered. Where there is background with no motif, the space is covered with a filling stitch. This background space should not be confused with the negative space that was discussed in the Design Concept section.

SCATTER EFFECT TECHNIQUE 1

Spaced random placement of stitches – single or double beads

This scatter effect technique is most frequently used to fill a background to set off the motif. It provides a backdrop with a very subtle movement. Where a mottled fabric is used for the ground, shadow effects are created with areas of light and dark.

In this technique single beads are applied randomly. Spacing between beads is fairly consistent and the beads are applied at random angles. It is correct that the background fabric will show through. Take care that beads do not line up or the gentle and light appearance intended will be lost.

Pin stitch after every 3–4 stitches.

Alternatively, stitches can be made with two beads which gives a slightly denser appearance.

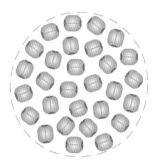

KITS

ENCHANTED

Page 24

Kit contains: Fabric with pre-printed design incl. hand-painted gilding, adhesive felt, card wallet frame, sewing threads, beads, metal thread and needles

JEWELS

Page 32

Kit contains: Fabric with pre-printed design, adhesive vinyl, fusible interfacing, glasses case frame, sewing threads, beads and needles

SHIPPO FLOWERS

Page 42

Kit contains: Fabric with pre-printed design, fusible interfacing, sewing threads, beads, metallic thread and needles

Note: Wooden box not included – available for separate purchase.

NOSHI

Page 50

Kit contains: Fabric, dressmaker's carbon, adhesive felt, fusible interlining and interfacing, sewing threads, magnets, beads, metal threads and needles

TROPICANA

Page 62

Kit contains: Fabric with pre-printed design incl. hand-painted colour and gilding, adhesive felt, zipped purse frame, sewing threads, beads, metal thread and needles

AFTER KANDINSKY

Page 74

Kit contains: Fabric with pre-printed design, fusible interlining and interfacing, adhesive felt, sewing threads, magnets, beads, metal thread and needles

POSH

Page 86

Kit contains: Fabric with pre-printed design, interfacings, fusible wadding, adhesive vinyl, adhesive felt, sewing threads, perlé cotton, fibre-fill, hexagonal box, beads, metal thread and needles

WAU BULAN

Page 98

Kit contains: Fabric with pre-printed design incl. colour and gilding, fusible interlining and interfacing, adhesive felt, sewing threads, magnetic bag closure, beads, metal thread and needles

GARDEN SYMPHONY

Page 108

Kit contains: Fabric with pre-printed design incl. hand-painted colour and gilding, adhesive felt, A5 folio frame with zip, sewing threads, beads, metal thread and needles

Author
Margaret Lee

Editor
Susan O'Connor

Assistant Editor
Ellaine Bronsert

Graphic Design
Lynton Grandison

Photography
Brendan Homan

Styling
Natalie Homan

Production Manager
Jessie Huber

Production Assistant
Willow Fry

Kit & Sourcing Manager
Sue Forrest

Studio Management
Kristian & Andrea Fleming

First released 2024

Published by:
Inspirations Studios Corporation Pty Ltd
PO Box 10177
Adelaide Business Hub
South Australia 5000
Australia
www.inspirationsstudios.com

Text, illustrations and projects
copyright © Margaret Lee 2024

Photography, design and layout
copyright © Inspirations Studios Corporation Pty Ltd 2024

The Art of Bead Embroidery | Japanese-Style 2
ISBN 978 0 6456407 3 1
© Copyright 2024
Inspirations Studios Corporation Pty Ltd

Printed & bound in China

INSPIRATIONS

For more of the world's most beautiful needlework
publications, please visit our website:
www.inspirationsstudios.com

MARGARET LEE
E M B R O I D E R Y

To discover more about Margaret Lee, her classes, touring
schedules, and range of products, please visit her website:
www.margaretlee.com.au